MULTICULTURAL EDUCATION, THE INTERNET, AND THE NEW MEDIA

MEDIA EDUCATION CULTURE TECHNOLOGY
Robert Muffoletto, Series Editor

Educational Technology: Critical and Reflective Practices
  Robert Muffoletto (ed.)

Multicultural Education, the Internet, and the New Media
  Robert Muffoletto and *Julie Horton* (eds.)

Social Learning from Broadcast Television
  Karen Swan, Carla Meskill, and *Steven DeMaio,* (eds.)

MULTICULTURAL EDUCATION, THE INTERNET, AND THE NEW MEDIA

edited by

Roberto Muffoletto
Appalachian State University

Julie Horton
Appalachian State University

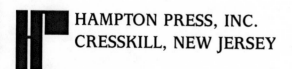

HAMPTON PRESS, INC.
CRESSKILL, NEW JERSEY

Printed in the United States of America

Library of Congress Cataloging-in-Publication Data

Multicultural education, the Internet, and the new media / [edited by] Roberto Muffoletto, Julie Horton.
    p.cm. -- (Media education culture technology)
    Includes bibliographical references and index.
    ISBN 1-57273-740-9 (casebound) -- ISBN 1-57273-741-7 (perfectbound)
    1. Internet in education. 2. Mass media in education. I. Muffoletto, Robert.
II. Horton, Julie.

    LC1099.M837 2007
    371.33'44678--dc22

                    2006033418

Cover art by Joe Orffeo

Hampton Press, Inc.
23 Broadway
Cresskill, NJ 07626

CONTENTS

1

THE INTERNET AND MULTICULTURAL EDUCATION

A Potential for Globalization

Roberto Muffoletto

Julie Horton

Throughout this book, the authors address issues related to the potential intersection of the Internet within a multicultural education framework. We seek to identify issues, visions, and potentials leading to new relationships centering on democratic practices, equity, and the social construction of knowledge and justice. This work is significant because of the impact of a digital culture on the day-to-day definitions of knowledge, and "the other," as well as its capacity to deliver curriculums on a global scale to an increasingly diverse population.

From our perspective, an education that is multicultural must deconstruct the management of gender, race, socioeconomic status (SES), and the historical nature of knowledge as normal practice. Thus, an education firmly rooted in this philosophy should be an ongoing process for each individual based on mutual respect of all cultures, whose goal is to increase the achievement of all students (AACTE, 1973; Banks, 1991, 1994, 2003; Bennett, 2003). At its best, multicultural education supports the development of identity, solidarity, critical thinking, and liberatory action (Ramsey, 1998). Banks (1995), believed an important goal of "multicultural teaching is to help students to understand how knowledge is constructed [to see] how cultural assumptions, frames of references, perspectives and the biases within a discipline influence the ways knowledge is constructed" (p. 11).

The challenge then is not only to prepare teachers who have multiple perspectives and are willing to reflect on their cultural biases, but also to have instructional systems and teacher educators who model this as well (Britzman, 1991).

Multicultural education must also be integrated into all areas of the curriculum and serve as an extension of activities and discussions vital to every aspect of learning (King et al., 1994). Therefore, an education, which is multicultural, is a counterdiscourse to the "ahistorical and nonconflicting" perception of knowledge a standardized curriculum may present. It is an education that is absent of "grand narratives" and dominant truths (Apple, 1990, 1996; Shor, 1992; Sleeter, 1996).

The emergence of a digital culture adds another element or level to our thinking concerning multicultural education in light of the developments in computer technology and systems development (the Internet). At present, students and teachers are not limited to computer media tools and stored content on a local or regional level. The Internet and the encoding or digitalization of data, accessed through a potentially global network, provides access to multiple "ways of knowing" and cultural frameworks. Digital culture links its members to each other and to a common encoded database, providing for the fluid exchange of ideas, representations, and points of view.

Living in a digital culture allows the possibility of developing a new sense of community. In this manner, digital culture begins to redefine community, knowledge, and practice by broadening perspectives and reconstructing the subjectivity of the individual and community. In short, an education that is multicultural within a digital culture has a potential to redefine that culture. Thus, the individual's identity becomes redefined within a much broader sense of the social world.

EDUCATIONAL TECHNOLOGY—
A BRIEF CONTEXT

We believe two concepts must be addressed under the umbrella of power, educational technology, and globalization. In terms of education, those in power will always impose on the haves from the have-nots. Thus, education can never be a "neutral assemblage of knowledge" (Taylor, 1994, p. 22) due to the mix of competing theories, ideologies, economics, and politics from educators, politicians, and society, which continuously shift and change.

Educational technology is not merely about the use of devices like computers and digital cameras by teachers and students to explore and remediate their world. Educational technology is about certainty; it is the placement of control and the centralization of power. It is important to consider the consumption of computers and media in education for the purpose of fostering efficiency and accountability while delivering a curriculum in an effective manner. Educational technology within a digital culture has the potential to deliver on a grand scale selected stories and myths concerning the world and the nature of being. Educational technology in very real ways deconstructs and reconstructs the individual in its own image.

The history of educational technology, like multicultural education, is a site of struggle and compromise. The struggle emerges from the use of media and computers to either deliver the official curriculum in controlled ways (systems approach) or the use of media and computers by teachers and students for creative and innovative work, changing the content and nature of "the" curriculum. The first centers on control of the process of schooling within the hands of the institution and those that benefit from it. The second falls within the minds and hearts of teachers and students. In a growing period of regimentation and control of the schooling experience, it becomes helpful to situate the field of educational technology within a historical context. It is through this history that we come to understand the control and dissemination of data and its interpretation into the schooling experience. We can safely say that what and how we know about the world, its history, and its people are controlled through various mediated and remediated experiences.

The field of educational technology, or as it also termed "*instructional technology*" has a rich and dynamic legacy within the history of schooling in the United States. Discourses concerning educational technology from a mainstream, commonsense perspective positions technology as a collection of devices. In the late 20th century, computers became analogous with the term *technology*, which separated it from media and other earlier devices. When educators speak of technology in education, or the integration of technology in education, they usually mean computers and supportive hardware—scanners, printers, graphic tablets, and digital cameras. Rarely do they refer to the structural relationship among hardware (devices), software (the content), and theories related to their use in learning and teaching environments.

Before 1940, the field of educational technology did not exist as we now understand it. The forerunner of technology in education was coined as *audiovisual aids*. Different from the dominant thinking concerning technology, audiovisual materials were thought of as an aid to the teacher in the delivery of the curriculum. Thus, the span of audiovisual instructional materials included photographs, cameras (still and moving), audio recordings and playback machines, phonographs, films, and other graphic and audio materials. Basic to understanding audiovisuals in education was its placement as an aid to teaching. The teacher was still central to the development of teaching materials and the dissemination (teaching) of the curriculum. In contrast, educational technology moved beyond the confines of being an aid to becoming the deliverer or interface to the curriculum (Muffoletto, 2001).

Thus, in the late 1960s, we find educational TV delivering the curriculum, taught by a master teacher. In the mid-1960s and through the 1970s, we find the emergence of individualized programs and kits designed to deliver the curriculum, positioning the teacher as a manager of the classroom rather than a teacher of the curriculum, making the program teacher safe. The instructional programs or kits contained all the elements needed to teach the curriculum from pre- and posttesting, the organization and presentation of the curriculum, and the summative evaluation of the student's performance. In a very important manner, the classroom teacher was being deskilled. At this historical point, we find the development and dissemination of educational programs that addressed the individual—SRA kits are a prime example of this development. The kit was the forerunner of the computer-delivered curriculum we wish to integrate into the schooling experience of the learner. In contemporary terms, the kit has become the integrated multimediated learning program delivered via the Internet or a CD-ROM. This distinction between aids and programs is important to consider when the content of the curriculum—the stories told to children and adults—is considered.

Educational technology as a field emerged after World War II. It was a field that merged engineering principals, neo-behaviorist learning theories, and the curriculum. The purpose and application of this melting pot was to solve problems and meet the needs of education as understood by those outside the classroom and education in general. Educational technology as a merging of systems theory, devices, and learning theory may be better thought of as being centered on a "science of certainty and control" over one that supports academic freedom and the empowerment of learners and teachers. Furthermore, the field did not consider any device as prime, but was centered on process. Thus, the emergence of contemporary views of educational technology as a process to achieve with certainty predefined outcomes, to solve educational needs, is based on instrumental rationality.

From this systems perspective, privileged devices and the function of computers evolved in education into the storage, retrieval, and display of a system for the delivery of the curriculum. Add to this the Internet, and you have a form for the dissemination of the curriculum and the evaluation of the learner on a global scale. Central to an analysis of the use of technology in education, is positioning it as a system of certainty over its objectifications as a computer or collection of devices.

To state again, educational technology is concerned with a systematic approach to the identification and solution of educational or instructional needs. What is at issue then is the data, the stories told through the system, both overt and covert—a system rooted in beliefs concerning science and progress, which constructs the individual not as historical subject, but as ahistorical object to be molded and formed to fit a predetermined construct. It is a system found on a global scale, with selected stories and tales that move beyond national borders and ethnocentric myths. It is a system, that attempts to construct with certainty the individual who will reproduce and maintain the system. By addressing issues related to globalization and power in relation to multicultural education, we may begin to redraw the horizon line.

GLOBALIZATION

What is at stake here is the framework for a definition of *globalization* in light of the possibilities and potential use of the Internet. Globalization may be considered from two broad polarizations—a color and white perspective if you wish. First, globalization may be framed as the work of Western rationalization and science, the growth of capitalism through the development of expanded markets, and the enhancement of an unskilled labor pool, in an effort to move developing Third World cultures into the modern world benefiting everyone. Second, globalization may be understood in a hegemonic framework where Western rationality and economic systems exploit a labor pool for the benefit of a few while planting the seeds of Western rationality and control. The effort here is to establish a common language and culture. Through globalization we would all become the same at critical levels. The Internet, as a tool for business, education, and socioeconomic transformation, enhancing the quality of life on a global scale, is framed through the lens of Western rationality, a market-driven economy, and competition.

In this light, the cultural traditions and the quality of life for millions of people are at risk. When critiquing the concept of globalization and the Internet, in light of a multicultural education, the question of benefit and privilege is of great importance: Who and what benefits from the expansion of the Internet to developed (meaning westernized) and developing countries? (It needs to be noted here that the concept of developing is from a Western perspective, where it is a commonsense notion that we have it right and that development is equal to progress.)

The Internet offers possibilities for communication and exchange that early modern devices could not. It is now possible that every citizen could potentially have access to an information network, education, and training on a global scale, as well as the environment to publish one's own story in the context of others. Through developing broadband systems, such as two-way satellite data transfer, every individual could be part of the global community. Issues related to equity of access and computer power, language, and cultural references need to be faced and addressed before such a vision could become common. The Internet and the new media systems offer to democratize technology.

In the end, those who define the nature and purpose of globalization will construct the cultural and social framework to benefit their perspective. How the horizon lines of a global economy, a global education system, and a global culture are drawn and maintained is of great importance to the conception of an education that is multicultural—one that recognizes a democratic, socially just, and connected world.

POWER

It may be helpful to understand digital culture, multicultural education, educational technology, globalization, and education in general within the framework of power. In this sense, Nilson (1998) pointed out, "[p]ower is not an institution, and not a structure. . . . It is the name that one attributes to a complex strategical situation in a particular society" (p. 64). Negotiating this terrain is difficult, and one must look at the notion of power controlling all these factors.

To reveal the ongoing power struggles within any institution, educators need to unpack the layers of power relationships among the processes of schooling, technology, globalization, and cultural identity by actively engaging the following questions: Who controls what is taught in schools? Whose knowledge is taught? What knowledge is valued? Whose interests does this knowledge serve? Who gets excluded as a result? Who is marginalized? Therefore, the knowledge acquired in school is "never neutral or objective but is ordered and structured in particular ways" (McLaren, 1989, p. 169).

Teachers have power in the classroom and, as such, have the authority and ability to value one type of knowledge and language over another. When teachers fail to question curricula and their relevance, or the ways schooling reproduces existing class, race, and gender relations in our society, they run the risk of conveying that they believe the existing inequalities in schools are justified (McLaren, 1989). However, this power is eroding as the use of educational technology is increasing and standardized curriculum and testing becomes commonplace (Muffoletto, 2001). As a profession, teachers are losing their authority in the classroom and their ability to teach in innovative and creative ways.

Teachers, as active participants and educational leaders, need to understand the role that schooling plays in joining knowledge and power so they can use their position to encourage the development of critical and active citizens. The basic values, beliefs, attitudes, and commitments that presently dominate the structure, content, and activities of schooling must be understood, because it is against this background that students and teachers encounter failure.

Tools provide society with advantages and solutions, but also dilemmas and concerns. Educational technology has provided only a few of these. At the same time, one of the goals of multicultural education has been to teach students to "have a flexible, not narrow, view of the world around them" (Gallagher, 1998, p. 24). It appears that the use of technology and globalization can assist us in doing just this by broadening our horizon lines and our understanding of self and others with broader historical and social contexts. The chapters included in this text continue this conversation and, in the end we hope, reveals other issues, questions, and context.

REFERENCES

AACTE. (1973). No one model American. *Journal of Teacher Education, 24,* 264-265.

Apple, M. (1990). *Ideology and curriculum* (2nd ed.). New York: Routledge.

Apple, M. W. (1996). *Cultural politics & education.* New York: Teachers College Press.

Banks, J. A. (1991). Multicultural education: Its effects on students' racial and gender role attitudes. In J. P. Shaver (Ed.), *Handbook of research on social studies teaching and learning* (pp. 459–469). New York: Macmillan.

Banks, J. A. (1994). *An introduction to multicultural education.* Boston: Allyn & Bacon.

Banks, J. A. (1995). Multicultural education: Historical development, dimensions, and practice. In J. A. Banks & C. A. McGee Banks (Eds.), *Handbook of research on multicultural education* (pp. 3–24). New York: Simon & Schuster Macmillan.

Banks, J. A. (2003). Multicultural education: Characteristics and goals. In J. A. Banks & C. A. McGee Banks (Eds.), *Multicultural education: Issues and perspectives* (4th ed., pp. 3-30). Boston: Wiley.

Bennett, C. I. (2003). *Comprehensive multicultural education: Theory and practice.* (5th ed.) Boston: Allyn & Bacon.

Britzman, D. P. (1991). *Practices makes practice.* Albany: State University of New York Press.

Gallagher, J. (1998). Multiculturalism at a crossroads. *The Education Digest, 63*(8), 23–28.

King, E. W., Chipman, M., & Cruz-Janzen, M. (1994). *Educating young children in a diverse society.* Boston: Allyn & Bacon.

McLaren, P. (1989). *Life in schools: An introduction to critical pedagogy in the foundations of education.* New York: Longman.

Muffoletto, R. (2001). The need for critical theory and reflective practices in educational technology. In R. Muffoletto (Ed.), *Education & technology: Critical and reflective practices.* Cresskill, NJ: Hampton Press.

Nilson, H. (1998). *Michel Foucault and the games of truth*. New York: St. Martin's Press.

Ramsey, P. G. (1998). *Teaching and learning in a diverse world*. New York: Teachers College Press.

Shor, I. (1992). *Empowering education: Critical teaching for social change*. Chicago: The University of Chicago Press.

Sleeter, C. E. (1996). *Multicultural education as social activism*. Albany: State University of New York Press.

Taylor, C. (1994). The politics of recognition In A. Gutman (Ed.), *Multiculturalism* (pp. 1-20). Princeton, NJ: Princeton University Press.

2

STUDENTS IN WONDERLAND

Voice, Identity, and New Realities Online

John Hollenbeck

Editor's note: One promise of the new digital media and the Internet is its ability to democratize education, communication, information, and technology. In this chapter, Hollenbeck leads the reader through an argument that calls for the democratization of learning environments, providing all learners a voice in their own education. The implications of this for education is great, for to democratize "voice" is to engage all learners in the contingency of knowing and to value all perspectives and worldviews as a foundational framework.

When the Internet first started to become a public medium, many saw it as a facilitator of democracy. The masses were to be given unlimited access to information, and communication was to be facilitated to an unprece-dented degree. Efforts were made to "wire" governments and allow all cit-izens a direct line to their elected officials. Congressional documents such as The Starr Report (http://thomas.loc.gov/icreport/) were cited as examples of public information becoming instantly available, thus creating a more informed public. A profound new world was opening to all cultures, learn-ing styles, and socioeconomic classes. All that was needed was access.

The concept of online learning was a large part of this vision. Online classes in the early 1990s were observed to be radically different from both the traditional classroom and previous distance learning efforts (Harasim, 1989). Because of its lack of traditional classroom cues, there was said to be a leveling of power in the online world. Teachers became facilitators and students full participants. With this leveling of power came an increase in learner autonomy. Students were observed to have taken responsibility for their learning and employed learning options that were personally relevant. Ultimately, many saw the promise of a truly democratic educational environment.

As with most educational technology revolutions, these promises have proved anything but inevitable. Currently, as academic institutions have increased implementation of online learning, the environment has been (re)turned into a "virtual classroom" where students are acting in a more "normal" student role. Using administrator-friendly names like "Blackboard" and "eCollege," learning management systems (LMS) prioritize the distribution of teacher-developed content over discussion and community-building activities. Much of the appeal of these systems is that they ease the posting of classroom materials, therefore allowing a lone professor to create online learning with a minimum of instructional design and/or technical help. The LMS seeks to make course creation efficient while retaining the traditional teacher-led priority; student involvement is, at best, an after thought.

There is then a tension between the early vision and the current implementation of online learning. The potential of an inclusive democratic medium has met with the reality of institutional priorities. The struggle online is to resist the seemingly inevitable subsumption of this new medium into the old institutional technology of learning. Wonderland is not gone, but access has been made more difficult. Yet the Internet remains the most accessible mass medium for creation and distribution of materials. Web pages are not nearly as hard to create and distribute as TV shows. It remains possible to form a mediated environment in a dynamic world of fluid locations, times, and identities.

Perhaps the key notion in this problem is the idea that technology determines possibilities. This may have roots in an overapplication of McLuhan's (1967) famous statement that "the medium is the message." Although the Internet certainly has definite attributes and deficiencies, its merely showing up did not automatically change education. In fact it acted more in accordance with Tyack and Tobin's (1994) notion that technologies tend to have their wings trimmed by the institution in which they are assimilated. Early in the use of online learning, it was not a significant part of academia's plans. But this has indeed changed, and so have the priorities of the medium.

CULTURE AND THE CURRENT LOCATION
OF ONLINE LEARNING

The demand for tertiary education is growing rapidly, far outstripping the socioeconomic will of most global societies. Universities find themselves with a glut of interested students, but no room to accommodate them (Tiffin & Rajasingham, 2003). The answers to this dilemma have come to many administrators—first distance education and now online learning. In Virginia, Old Dominion University's president offered to accommodate an additional 10,000 students via distance learning and online education in an effort to meet the state's overload of demand (Daniel, 2003). In California, a major effort was initiated by the California State University system to create a "virtual university" (Thompson, 1996). The appeal is understandable from a business standpoint; there is comparatively little cost in mounting televised and virtual courses and a great potential for unlimited amounts of students, especially when compared with building new facilities. Online learning has been combined with distance education as the "wave of the future" to extend the university. There is no concern about to whom it is being extended, just the accommodation of more customers. For most campuses, online learning is the most cost-effective way to increase student numbers.

The current state of online learning is dominated by Web-based applications such as Blackboard and WebCT. These LMS are based on bulletin-board interactions common in earlier text-based technologies such as FirstClass or Lotus LearingSpace. There exists a prepared structure for the posting of various kinds of material, test creation, and student interaction. They also add features that are designed to assist an instructor in making materials available to students. These LMS are World Wide Web-based, making it possible to code messages in HTML and include graphics and sound in a limited way.

Interaction in online learning environments is based on asynchronous postings, where students and instructors converse by making a post and then responding, forming threads. Although some limited formatting of these posts is possible, most of the interaction is done in plain text. Therefore, it is a culture of words—English words. Often non-native English speakers have greater difficulty in American online courses because of the need to constantly compose written text. This problem compounds in synchronous chat environments, where conversants type messages in a rapid and often disconnected pace. A great deal of slang is also part of synchronous interaction.

Current implementations of LMS often do not attempt to increase student role—in fact they both view and seek to maintain the practice of the didactic classroom. The teacher is clearly defined and (in many implementations) is the only one allowed to perform administrative and posting functions. Students are generally given a less significant role, unable to create discussion forums, post documents, and generally participate in the creation of the class. The priority on access leads to virtual classrooms, not collaborative environments. Virtual classrooms may try to be different from the didactic classroom, but in practice they rarely are.

SUBSUMPTION OF TECHNOLOGY IN A TECHNOLOGY

The possibilities for inclusive democratic learning are becoming more diminished as an increasing number of universities see online learning as a way to accommodate and/or expand student enrollment. The clear priority of academic institutions is access to traditionally qualified students. Online learning is felt to be an acceptable replacement for the classroom and a pedagogical alternative to the current practice of higher education. Typically, administrators feel that online learning is the "wave of the future" and that "the train has left the station," so it is time to act. There is little encouragement to ask about academic or social consequences of such a move.

This is in line with the typically American concept of distance learning as a way to increase access to learning. The term *virtual classroom* has become associated with both online and televised media, and actions in these environments are closely aligned to the workings of the school. Europeans see distance and online learning primarily as a pedagogical extension. New kinds of educational institutions, such as the British Open University, operate in vastly different ways from the brick and mortar school. Here school is altered to the cultural realities of individuals not able to access a traditional university. In America, it is a problem of access, whereas in Europe it is a problem of pedagogics (see Peters, 1998).

As this happens, the early optimism about democratic online environments is vanishing as the institution has discovered online learning and made it conform to its practices. Simple discussion boards are being replaced by single LMS chosen not by faculty, but rather administration and technical support. Online learning is now about preservation and expansion of market, not change in educational practice. But if this is the current trend, it is not inevitably so. The Internet has proved to be hard to control.

DEMOCRACY

Democracy may be defined most broadly as containing two elements. In almost all cases it is a form of popular self-government. The populace most typically votes in a popular election to choose representatives and pass laws. Majority rules in these cases, and the "will of the people" is heard throughout the actions of government (Wiebe, 1995). The uncontrolled rule of a majority was greatly feared in democracy's infancy, however, especially after the events of the French Revolution (Abramson et al., 1988). This fear led to the checks and balances and other constitutional limitations intended to preserve the rights of both individuals and minorities from the plebiscitic will of a simple majority. The initial practice of American democracy, especially at the national level, was greatly distanced from the electorate. Only in the mid-19th century did the selection of government officials start to become an act of public will (Johnson, 1991). Still, in some regulated way, popular self-rule is a consistent feature of any democracy.

Combined with democracy's universal quality of social self-governance is a secondary quality that reflects the social context in which it develops. The more formal democracies of Europe retain a class-consciousness to guard against loss of culture, for instance. In America, this secondary feature is drawn from the country's tradition of individualism—the right of every citizen to control his and [later] her own future (Wiebe, 1995). American democracy developed from an American frontier that knew none of the limits of Europe and was burdened with none of its restrictions. Almost aggressively, American democracy became a practice of free White men viewed as equals and acting the same. The rootlessness of society created a freedom of movement that transcended class structure and tore down hierarchies of ruling power (Wiebe, 1995). Also, the endless frontier created a sense of endless possibility—a feature that was to have a profound effect upon the development of an American philosophy (Campbell, 1995).

American democracy, then, may be seen as a struggle between individual and social needs. Some see a loss of meaningful community as threatening democracy's survival (Lasch, 1995). Others see a loss of individual rights within a morass of government regulation (Wiebe, 1995). It is the struggle for balance between these two qualities that can be held responsible for the creation and practice of many differing kinds of educational democracy. Starting with Horace Mann, the importance of education to democracy has long been recognized, because democracy is a way of life that replaces the legitimacy of outside authority, be it monarch or god, with the informed will of the populace (Kliebard, 1986). This association has led to a number of writings about how democracy and education should be associated. The following four short scenarios are intended to illustrate those ideals.

DEMOCRACY IN THE CONTEXT
OF THE CLASSROOM

School 1: All have the right to participate in the governance of the school. Texts, lessons, and priorities are all the result of a truly genuine effort to allow students to be involved in decisions that affect their lives. Their process is a struggle against the priority of institutional efficiency and hierarchical power that mark the dominant tradition of the American school; racism, injustice, poverty, and concentrated power are all confronted and stood against. This democracy stands up against all oppressors (Beane & Apple, 1995).

School 2: Concern is given to using the right amount of democracy in the classroom. Participation based on students' choice in the subjects to be taught is seen as desirable, but there is a fear that too much of this will lead to chaos, as well as inviting raw cultural problems, such as racism, to become evident. The importance of the internal structure of schooling is set against concerns of democratic participation; a balance is sought between both for education to continue (Grundy, 1987; Gutmann, 1987).

School 3: Curriculum is employed out of the child's experience and interest. The school endeavors to be a small version of the community, but one where experimentation is safe and the dangers of life are controlled. It maneuvers between the extremes of educational debate. Students are not blindly subjected to subject matter in a formulaic manner, yet they are neither allowed to follow their own interests nor are they rewarded for mere attraction to certain educational ideals. The teachers act on opportunities as they arise from the students' interests within the framework of the classroom lessons. The teachers are also very tired, burdened by a great deal of responsibility that comes from being the intellectual intermediaries between an avalanche of educational theory and its application to their very active students (Dewey, 1938, 1956).

School 4: Students at this school attend through the democratic right of the parents to choose a proper school that reflects their values. It is based on the principles that every young American needs an education with a solid academic core, including knowledge, skills, democratic values, and a healthy dose of cultural literacy. It is designed and operated to meet the

needs of its consumers, rather than the interests of its pro-
ducers. One way this has been brought about is through civil-
ian control of key policy decisions (Bloom, 1987; Hirsch,
1987; Ravitch, 1983).

Each of these schools is intended to illustrate a way in which democracy is used within educational rhetoric and practice. They also serve to
illustrate different flavors of American democracy and a shifting of priorities between social and individual rights. Abramson et al. (1988) identified
three forms of democracy that may be illustrated in the earlier examples.
The first, a plebiscitic democracy, is concerned with individual autonomy
and its priority of providing as many people as possible the freedom to participate in governance. Perhaps a good summation of this concept is that it
is a simple *majority rules* political group—the more who can participate,
the better. This type of system threatens both individuals and minorities
with being run over by the majority (Ess, 1996).

Perhaps School 4 is the best illustration of this usage. In all cases of policy and choice, it is considered democratic for parents to be able to choose
where their child goes to school and what that child is taught. This *vote with
the feet* is based on concerns for our country as a democracy and identified
needs for its preservation. Thus, terms such as *cultural literacy* are used to
denote the kinds of skills that will be necessary for our society to succeed
(Bloom, 1987; Hirsch, 1987). Each individual is called on to join the melting pot and become one nation; education here provides the heat for the
pot.[1]

A second form of democracy is labeled *communitarian* (Abramson et
al., 1988). It is the common good of the group that is most important,
rather than individual freedom and majority rule. Participation in community life is held in highest regard. Here a participant would seek to be
involved with public meetings, advocacy for desired positions, and use this
work for the common good of the community. Although seen as more
desirable than plebiscitic democracy, communitarian democracy still carries a danger of the exclusion of minority communities based on the
strength of that majority.

School 1 may be seen to exhibit the characteristics of a communitarian democracy. This manifests itself in a somewhat antagonistic manner,
pitting the *us* of the underclasses based on racial, gender, and economic
factors against the *them* of the ruling power elite, most often characterized

---

[1]Of course I am avoiding a number of larger debates with this summary. That this
view is most surely held by the Right, with its conservative and Eurocentric agenda, is understood and accepted here.

as the Right (Hostetler, 1995). Democracy in the instance of this school is used in essence to call the bluff of those in power. Although the rights of the group are upheld, they are defended in a manner that clearly defines an absolute right and wrong in the context of the school's community. Schools 2 and 3 also exhibit characteristics of this communitarian form of democracy, although in a less confrontational manner. Groups in these cases are identified, but freely interact with one another.

The final category is that of pluralist democracy. While allowing for the kinds of competitions and coalitions among different communities that act to offset plebiscitic domination, the greater goal of this form of democracy is to ensure that all groups are given a voice in the greater community in which they are a part. The expansion of the communitarian ideal with a transcendence of competition that features only winners and losers ensures voice and power for all members of a society (Ess, 1996). This priority is most assuredly lacking in School 4. It seeks to form us into one nation through the teaching of a common culture and the use of rigid standards for achievement. The degree to which pluralistic action is a commitment is also questionable in School 1, given its confrontational flavor. Schools 2 and 3 have the potential for this kind of democracy, although it is not assured in either case.

Each of these categories contains elements that may be considered recognizable in conceptions and uses of the term *democracy*. But each is also unique from the others, containing some priority that radically sets it apart from the other examples. This serves as an example of the confusion that surrounds democratic claims and actions, and it challenges any who venture into this arena to be clear about their intentions. With this in mind, let us turn to a consideration of voice.

VOICE

For many, the creation of the Internet has led to the formation of any number of possible worlds. The popular press is filled with works showing this new medium as a place of alternative community—one where communication and negotiation would take place in a new and equitable manner (assuming one owned or had access to a connected computer). Once online, voice and identity are seen as negotiable. One's identity or culture can be re-created any number of times (Rheingold, 1993; Turkle, 1995).

Pioneers in the educational uses of computer conferencing often cited results such as more equitable conversational relations between participants, including teacher and student, dominant and shy personalities, and urban and rural participants as reasons for an increase in democracy. I

have examined questions about the democratic nature of computer conferencing in education by studying the online interactions between
instructors and students (Hollenbeck, 1998). It seemed to me at that time
students were able to interact at a different level than was typical in a
classroom. They interacted with instructors as peers, exhibiting and
empowered voice necessary for democratic action. I concluded that the
new medium had effectively removed traditional classroom cues and had
thus created a blank slate, which these students used to create a democratic learning environment.

It has now become apparent that these early findings are truer for
those who easily find voice in the printed English language. Bulletin boards
favor those who can clearly state their points in no more than two para-
graphs. Indeed there is a style to writing for the Web that must be considered in LMS interactions. The current low fidelity of the computer monitor
makes reading long passages uncomfortable. Writers are encourage to create "scannable" content that follows journalistic conventions of brevity
and point development. Only a few can develop voice inside a 50-word
utterance.

Despite this, two main advantages have long been touted for online
interaction. One is that it allows the "shy to speak," as it is felt the relative
anonymity of online posting allows more introverted personalities to interact. For those introverts comfortable with expressing themselves in text,
this has surely been true. Yet these sorts of epiphanies are not all that common; few introverts bloom online.

The second advantage is seen as the ability to reflect on one's response
to a posting before interacting. Again this may be a limited benefit, but in
practice most online participants read and respond in one motion. There
may be simple revisions along the way, but online threads tend to read like
conversations "off the cuff" as opposed to print debates.

So the development of voice is presently limited to those comfortable
with text expression in most cases. The use of graphics and video remains
peripheral at best, and these come with their own high technical costs.
Most LMS limit the options for those wishing to interact online to the text
bulletin boards. Student voice, then, is more a result of instructional design
than media attribute.

NEW REALITIES

The traditional American school and university have preserved a delivery
model of education for most of this century. Decisions about what is to be
learned when have been left in the hands of educational authorities—

teachers, school boards, university committees, and so forth. The student's role has, in the barest sense, been to learn this knowledge in the form given to him or her and be able to replicate it in tests and papers.

Key to the preservation of this model of learning is the medium of the classroom. In most traditional schools, rows of desks are placed facing the front of the room. There the instructor is given sole access to those materials used to present content, be they a blackboard, chart, overhead, or networked computer. The message of this media is to consume—to be perhaps an active listener, but to indeed listen and absorb. Students learn to take the same place in the room and perform the rituals of the classroom to the extent they are forced to.

Attempts to change this medium, this priority on teaching as telling, have largely failed to this day. Reformers generally have grossly underestimated the robustness of the institution of school (Kliebard, 1986). Its structure acts to inhibit any attempts at changing practice, usually by placing responsibility for any reform squarely on the instructor's shoulder. New technologies are routinely brought into the institution with great promise of reform, only to find themselves subsumed by the hegemonic inertia of the established institution (Tyack & Tobin, 1994).

Democratic education involves a reallocation of that authority to all participants (Gutmann, 1987). Students become actors who are given the political right and responsibility to be involved with teachers and administrators in curricular decisions. Perhaps *responsibility* is the strongest term here, for in removing the authority of the teacher from the classroom a more active role is defined for the student. This emancipatory action carries with it the need for involved action.

Primary to the development of this democratic environment is the ability of each student's voice to be heard. Here is where media is indeed the message. In early studies, it was found that students tended to act in a democratic manner (Hollenbeck, 1998), but these were locations that consisted primarily of message lists. The client software (e.g., FirstClass) presented the viewer with message lists and folders that contained more messages. In other words, the priority of this implementation was the facilitation of interaction. Although content could be distributed, it was always done so in the context of a message that could be responded to.

But times have greatly changed since then. The first online courses were generally taught by individual professors who informally wanted to try it out. Their efforts largely "flew under the radar" of the institution. Although valued as an interesting anomaly, little attention was paid to them until the arrival of the commercial Internet. Then progress was measured by the use of this new medium. Online learning became a market, and there were suddenly profits to be made.

The message of Blackboard (Bb) is quite different from early packages, and it is typical of the current LMS. If student interactions are key to democratic learning environments, then the message of Bb is a return to monarchy. Conversation takes place in deeply buried forums that exist in isolation from course content. In most implementations, only the teacher is allowed to create new forums, and students must live with those choices.

Blackboard offers numerous administrative advantages, such as an ability to communicate with campus databases. It is sold as a turn-key solution that requires little involvement of technical personnel. Certainly, those institutions that attempted to make their own LMS welcomed this finished product.

Most important, Bb looks like school. The name speaks volumes of the priority of this LMS. Instructors are given premade areas to post content of various intentions—from syllabi to computer-graded exams. The entire administration of the class is reserved for the instructor only. Student contributions are limited to the premade discussion forums. Although there is an ability for students to create a personal home page, most campuses have disabled this function due to FERPA and/or legal concerns.

Of primary importance is the claim of Bb and other LMS to be easy to use for the instructor, and consistent for the user. This ease of use comes with greatly limited flexibility for how the course is created. This limitation grows if the instructor is not supported in course creation and/or has limited Web-authoring skills. In most cases, an instructor is given a workshop or two and is then invited to "move" his or her classroom materials online. The Bb structure acts as a faithful replicant of the classroom and a preserver of its roles.

WONDERLAND

The machine is valuable only after the real work is done. (Davies, 1997, p. 170)

If truly inclusive educational environments are to be created using online learning, then the emphasis needs to change from a concentration on what the technology allows to what education needs. In other words, technology must be made to foster educational diversity, rather than education adapting itself to the constraints of LMS. Institutional requirements such as registration and maintenance need to be honored, but not be the end in which the software is designed. Above all, online learning must be seen as a pedagogical problem first, not a way to extend the classroom. Distance education in Europe is more a pedagogical issue; there the focus is on how the medium changes the way education is conducted. Peters (1998) went so far as to claim that video conferencing is not distance education because pedagogically it remains rooted in time and place, even if there is more than one place.

Focusing on pedagogics gives interesting possibilities, including the development of environments that encourage democratic learning. Some, such as Pepperdine University, are experimenting with text-based virtual realities in which students are co-creators of their environments (Talley, 1997). Here both synchronous and asynchronous interactions can take place, and there is a great deal of flexibility in creating online learning. These online worlds become playgrounds for identity as well (Turkle, 1995).

The Web does offer intriguing possibilities for those willing to take on the challenge of learning to program it or to find one grant that funds hiring such people. Work in parallel disciplines such as Computer Supported Collaborative Work (CSCW) begins with the priority for facilitating interaction and collaboration (Greif, 1988). These are the things of democracy, where each individual is able to fully participate in the creation of knowledge. These are the rewards for those who dedicate time and resources to going beyond what the typical institution is providing. It takes a great deal of time, but perhaps here true change in education will take place.

CONCLUSION

Democratic learning environments require certain conditions in which they can flourish. Key is the ability of all participants to express themselves freely, share information, create learning situations, and exercise autonomy. Early in the implementation of online learning, there was a naive belief that the technology alone would make such environments an inevitability. Over the past decade, experience has proved that not to be the case. Online learning is now an institutional priority, and those features that do not support traditional learning are marginalized and discarded. Yet the computer remains a flexible and accessible medium. What is needed is for educators to drive the design and implementation of diverse and accessible learning environments that have a priority for all students.

REFERENCES

Abramson, J. B., Arterton, F. C., & Orren, G. R. (1988). *The electronic commonwealth: The impact of new media technologies on democratic politics.* New York: Basic Books.

Beane, J. A., & Apple, M. W. (1995). The case for democratic schools. In M. W. Apple & J. A. Beane, *Democratic schools* (pp. 1–25). Alexandria, VA: Association for Supervision and Curriculum Development.

Bloom, A. (1987). *The closing of the American mind.* New York: Simon & Schuster.

Campbell, J. (1995). *Understanding John Dewey: Nature and cooperative intelligence.* Chicago: Open Courts.

Daniel, S. (2003). *University proposes adding 10,000 students by 2008.* Accessed August 18, 2004, at http://www.odu.edu/ao/instadv/vol32issue13/news.htm# 10000.

Davies, R. (1997). *The merry heart: Reflections on reading, writing and the world of books.* New York: Viking.

Dewey, J. (1938). *Experience and education.* New York: Macmillan.

Dewey, J. (1956). *The child and the curriculum and the school and society.* Chicago: University of Chicago Press.

Ess, C. (1996). The political computer: Democracy, CMC, and Habermas. In C. Ess (Ed.), *Philosophical perspectives on computer-mediated communication* (pp. 197–230). Albany: State University of New York Press.

Greif, I. (1988). *Computer-supported cooperative work: A book of readings.* San Mateo, CA: Morgan Kaufmann.

Grundy, S. (1987). *Curriculum: Product or praxis.* Philadelphia, PA: Falmer.

Gutmann, A. (1987). *Democratic education.* Princeton, NJ: Princeton University Press.

Harasim, L. (1989). On-line education: A new domain. In R. Mason & A. Kaye (Eds.), *Mindweave: Communication, computers and distance education* (pp. 50–62). Elmsford, New York: Pergamon.

Hirsch, E. D. (1987). *Cultural literacy: What every American needs to know.* Boston: Houghton-Mifflin.

Hollenbeck, J. (1998). Democracy and computer conferencing. *Theory Into Practice, 37*(1), 38-45.

Hostetler, K. (1995). Getting serious about the questions of democracy. *Educational Theory, 45*(1), 101–117.

Johnson, P. (1991). *The birth of the modern.* New York: HarperCollins.

Kliebard, H. M. (1986). *The struggle for the American curriculum 1893–1958.* London: Routledge & Kegan.

Lasch, C. (1995). *The revolt of the elites and the betrayal of democracy.* New York: W.W. Norton.

McLuhan, M. (1967). *The medium is the massage.* New York: Random House.

Peters, O. (1998). *Learning and teaching in distance education.* London: Kogan Page.

Ravitch, D. (1983). *The troubled crusade: American education, 1945–1980.* New York: Basic Books.

Rheingold, H. (1993). *The virtual community.* New York: HarperPerennial.

Talley, S. (1997). EdTech does it online at Pepperdine University. *Technological Horizons in Education, 24*(10), 69–71.

Thompson, J. (1996, May). *The California Virtual University.* Paper presented at the 11th annual DET/CHE conference, Los Angeles, CA.

Tiffin, J., & Rajasingham, L. (2003). *The global virtual university.* London: RoutledgeFalmer.

Turkle, S. (1995). *Life on the screen: Identity in the age of the internet.* New York: Simon & Schuster.

Tyack, D. B., & Tobin, W. (1994). The "grammar" of schooling: Why has it been so hard to change? *American Educational Research Journal, 31*(3), 453–479.

Wiebe, R. H. (1995). *Self-rule: A cultural history of American democracy.* Chicago: University of Chicago Press.

3

PROMETHEUS UNBOUND

Technology and the Spiritual Marketplace in Education

Davin Carr-Chellman

Alison A. Carr-Chellman

Editor's note: Carr-Chellman and Carr-Chellman address a topic often left outside the traditional venues of multicultural education, and for the most part public education in the United States. What they refer to as a *spiritual marketplace* brings new pressures to the public sphere, especially schooling. They argue that we need to move beyond mere topical dispensing of information and comparative contexts of religion to the use of technology to engage learners in diverse ways of understanding the human experience.

New technologies have brought and are bringing us closer and closer together. It is now cliché that this increased access has changed the way we live our lives, but there are some important truths behind the cliché, especially as educators are pressured to adopt new and emerging technologies as a panacea to systemic challenges. The dialogue that has developed around this important topic has neglected to include the deep and lasting effects of new and emerging technologies on the way we understand and approach religion in the public sphere, not the least of which is the public space we call schools. It is not an overstatement to say that this neglect is a kind of "giant white elephant in the middle of the room" considering the central role that religion and religious differences play in world events.

Clearly, the giant elephant can no longer be ignored, and technology has forced the issue. New and emerging technologies—part and parcel of the increasing rationalization of our society—have had the ironic effect of making religion and religious differences more prevalent and important. A spiritual marketplace has been introduced that is both liberating for the many seekers and scholars among us and also troubling for the contemporary guardians of secular and religious orthodoxy. The unexamined sociological effect of this spiritual marketplace is a generation of youth caught between an empowering but dangerous onslaught of information and a fearful but well-intentioned cohort of teachers, leaders, and mentors. The net effect is an unhealthy learning environment informed more by unstated and unrecognized phobias than by responsible and well-informed guidance. This situation is like the unbinding of Prometheus, whose intention was to provide a wealth of godlike resources for human progress, the success of which was superceded only by the irresponsibility of those most able to appropriately shape the use of those resources.

Based on our description of this unprecedented and uncomfortable situation, we argue that responsible educators will abandon their orthodoxy, whether it be secular or religious, and start to facilitate communication and engagement between and among religious traditions. This chapter addresses the ways in which technology can be used to truly engage the healing nature of religion in education. It addresses some difficult topics; religion in public schools alone is a tough discussion. So, reader beware, what you find in this chapter may offend or upset, but we promise it will engage. The chapter lays out the allegory of Prometheus more clearly as a starting point to discuss the unleashing of spirituality and technology within education. Next, we turn to a discussion of the ways in which traditional religious institutions have lost their power in postmodern society. A careful explication of the healing nature, the ecologically healing nature, of religion establishes the need to truly engage religious diversity in our schools.

THE BINDING OF PROMETHEUS

The story of Prometheus is a fitting allegory to understand the relationship that currently exists between technology and religion, especially as that relationship has developed in schools. According to Greek mythology, Prometheus stole fire from the Olympian gods to empower the mortal race of humans. Zeus, the most powerful Olympian, had plans for creation, which included the quick extinction of the primitive human race, declaring that knowledge and divine gifts would only bring misery to the sorry lot. Despite Zeus' intentions, Prometheus took pity on the mortals, giving them all sorts of gifts: brickwork, woodworking, telling the seasons by the stars, numbers, the alphabet, yoked oxen, carriages, saddles, ships, and sails. The list of gifts was extensive, but it was really the gift of divine fire that unleashed a flood of human inventiveness, productivity, and, most of all, reverence for the divine source of all these wonderful creations.

The rapidly developing mortals had surrounded Olympus with culture, art, and literacy, revealing to Zeus his betrayal at the hands of Prometheus. In his fury, Zeus commanded Hepheistos to shackle Prometheus to the side of a crag, high in the Caucasus Mountains, where he would remain until Zeus calmed. Every day, Prometheus would be tormented by Zeus' eagle as it tore into his immortal flesh, trying to devour his liver. Each night would mend the torn flesh, allowing the eagle to begin anew its gruesome task at dawn.

Given this myth, the characterization of Prometheus is usually of a naive God full of hubris and arrogance, so dim in perspective as to steal from the gods to enlighten mortal creatures. This is why Mary Shelley, the author of *Frankenstein*, subtitled her book *The Modern Prometheus*. Prometheus provided, in the literal sense of the word, technology that empowered humans to accomplish Olympian tasks, sometimes to their detriment when left without guidance. Prometheus was bound—shackled and tied—to a rock as punishment for adding new human pretense to the burden of Zeus' responsibility.

Certainly, Prometheus was devastated at the prospect of spending eternity bound to his daily torture, but even more he was saddened that the Olympians, especially Zeus, had lost touch with their hearts, their compassion, their empathy, and their benevolence; the vulnerable and dependent human race suffered because of the self-indulgent and misguided behavior of the guardians of Mount Olympus. For Prometheus, this abuse signaled the abdication of their right to rule.

A MODERN ABDICATION

The gods of Olympus carry little weight in the 21st century, but clearly our times bear witness to Olympians of a different sort. Every day the fact is made clearer that the guardians of orthodoxy (small "o")—both religious and secular—are abdicating their right to rule. The lesson for us is not that we are punished for stealing the fire of the gods, but that the keys to spiritual, scientific, and human evolution are often bound as tightly as Prometheus; bound by insecure yet influential figures of authority, lest the walls of Olympus—the walls of orthodoxy—crumble. Our religious and educational institutions are structured to separate, isolate, and discriminate; the ostensible goal of this structure is to understand and clarify the world. The undeclared net effect, however, is to separate and protect the known from the unknown, the safe from the delinquent, the inside from the outside, and the pure from the tainted. Our religious and educational institutions have become, instead of forces for individual empowerment and social agency, a gentrified gendarme of mediocrity. The guardians of orthodoxy govern the expression and recognition of matters of ultimate concern according to dogma—religious *and* secular dogma; dogma that is deeply discordant with sociological, political, scientific, technological, and religious reality. The walls they have created, depend on, and protect reflect *their* fear more than *our* reality. We live, as Eck (20010 said in "a new religious America," where the traditional boundaries and walls have become permeable at least and inconsequential at most. These are the same boundaries and walls in which our cultural institutions have invested so heavily.

In the United States, the religious landscape *is* new and, based on its characteristics, is best described as a spiritual marketplace. Quite literally, people go "church shopping" or, more subtly, a Hindu woman falls in love with a Muslim man, or an evangelical Christian becomes Catholic in college and wants to marry a Jew. At the same time, a new breed of religious fundamentalism has grown up around the spiritual marketplace, intent on building higher the walls that segregate. These scenarios represent something new on the horizon, something for which our institutions and professionals are profoundly ill prepared. Our religious and educational institutions and the people who lead them are unable to cope with the advent of the spiritual marketplace and the technology that propels it. In this new religious America, *Prometheus is unbound, only our institutions have not yet realized this fact*; or if they have realized this fact, they are resisting it to our individual and collective detriment. The danger of this ignorance is both stunted social and spiritual evolution and irrelevant religious and educational institutions.

Religion as Ecological Healing

Just as the gift of fire propelled human development, spirituality and its multiplicity of material manifestations are core components to making the world a better place—albeit neglected core components. In the secular and civic realms, religion is something to be feared, denigrated, or, at least, deemed inconsequential to earning a living, but in the 21st century, we ignore religion at great cost. Religion, above all else, is a human activity. It is as much an extension of our needs and desires as music, sport, and sex, for example. "It is," as others have said about philosophy, "an undertaking, a 'doing,' something that we engage in and undergo" (Stuhr, 2000, p. 435). As such, it is a product of our lives, the result of a whole nexus of events that are neither explainable as to their coincidence nor determinable as to their results. Religion is also an exceptionally divisive element as far as human activities are concerned, engulfing us more often than not in acts of condemnation and regrettably dogmatic visions of divine justice. The living out of our love of God, to give religion a decidedly Augustinian definition and tone,[1] finds many of us engaged in atrocious acts of hatred. Why, then, resurrect this monster?

In light of the collapse of reason culminating in the loss of the World Trade Center, thousands of lives, and the innocence of a nation, but propelled by religion, why not jettison this topic into the dustbin of history? The fact is, we engage it because we must, now more than ever. Religion *is* a product of our experience: It is part of the tapestry of our lives and, as such, is inescapable, whatever its form. In addition to (or part of) its inescapability is its incredible diversity; capturing cultures, trends, and attitudes as well or better than any photograph or motion picture. This richness is caught, however, on the bridge of a ship of fools: in plain sight of everyone, but sequestered and removed from the destination of most importance. It is a richness that should be embraced, appreciated, and understood, not hidden, scorned, and feared. As educators, it is our choice: Prometheus *is* unbound and our children have at their fingertips, through technology, the information to create either generations of relationship-oriented humanitarians or generations of isolationist ideologues.

We have always ignored our responsibility in this area, and there is solid evidence—anecdotally through community and world events and scientifically through rigorous research—that we are guilty of malicious neglect: Our inactivity has resulted in significant harm to the world community. Studies of intergroup relations among young people indicate that one-shot or limited exchanges rarely result in reduction of bias or prejudice and may, in fact, exacerbate stereotypes and animosity (Cotton, 1993). Extend this research to the sound-bite information dispensation style of the Internet and other electronic resources and it is clear that our children need and deserve guidance and interaction around issues of religious difference and multifaith engagement.

Certainly, there are concrete steps we can take to improve this situation, the first of which is a change in perspective. Religion is part of the modern human fire that Prometheus first brought to us at the dawn of time, and technology is a significant piece of Prometheus' modern unbinding. Given this scenario, we are morally obligated, lest we abdicate our rule, to nurture and educate forthcoming generations in the humanizing potential

---

[1] See John D. Caputo's (2001) *On religion.*

of our deep religious diversity. When understood this way, religion is about healing—healing that is powerful not because of its transcendence beyond differences, but because of its immanence within and embrace of differences. Religion must be discussed and confronted, analyzed, and understood because religion approached this way makes religion about healing.

When differences in faith traditions and religious sensibilities rear their ugly heads to contribute to the already massive pain and injustice of our world, we are reminded not only of the complexity of this realm of human experience, but also of the strange and varied ways that uncertainty and fear can overtake our consciousness. Ever present in our minds is the precariousness of life—the pain of the vicissitudes of our respective and mutual existences. Jaspers (1957) captured this shape-shifting characteristic of our lives very clearly:

> As compared with man (sic) in previous eras, man today has been uprooted, having become aware that he exists in what is but a historically determined and changing situation. It is as if the foundations of being had been shattered. . . . We live in a moment, a flux, a process, in virtue of which changing knowledge enforces a change in life; and in turn, changing life enforces a change in the consciousness of the knower. This movement, this flux, this process, sweeps us into the whirlpool of unceasing conquest and creation, of loss and gain, in which we painfully circle, subject in the main to the power of the current, but able now and then to exert ourselves within a restricted sphere of influence. For we do not only live in a situation proper to mankind at large, but we experience this situation as it presents itself in specific historical circumstances, issuing out of a previous situation and progressing towards a subsequent one. (pp. 2–3)

Jaspers sounded a somber tone—the precariousness of life is a heavy burden—but gestures toward a moment of hope that is part of each and every one of us: He called it "a restricted sphere of influence," but we are more sanguine, calling that moment of hope "the community." We are with Buber (1947) as he voiced the religious dimensions of community, the moment of hope and of healing in our sea of flux:

> We expect a theophany of which we know nothing but the place, and the place is called community. In the public catacombs of this expectation there is no single God's Word which can be clearly known and advocated, but the words delivered are clarified for us in our human situation of being turned to one another. There is no obedience to the coming one without loyalty to his creature. To have experienced this is our way. (p. 7)

This business of living is tough, and the way out of our predicament is not clear, in fact we seem to be sinking deeper into the muck. The irony of contemporary human existence is profound: There are more of us closer together than ever before, and technology offers us more and better ways to communicate than ever before, but we have never seemed less in touch and aware. Adding fuel to this fire is the apparent failure of our religious traditions to contribute in any meaningful way to the amelioration of these problems. Truth be told, it seems that religion contributes more to division than melioration, more to exaggerate these problems than to heal them.

Yet our frustration need not be so great, our angst not so prominent, and our path not so confused. Our religious traditions need not be a point of tension to be avoided as we endeavor to persevere in cross-cultural understanding. Instead they need to be more integral to this endeavor. Jasper's concern for the uprootedness of modern existence and the move-ment, flux, and process into which we are swept is genuine. Yes, we are constantly encountering voids and chasms in the wake of simply making our way through life, day in, day out. We know this fact on the individual level certainly, but also on the communal level. This is why Buber was so interested in the community: "The words delivered are clarified for us in our human situation of being turned to one another. There is no obedi-ence to the coming one without loyalty to his creature." His description is of a religious community, a community about healing—about ameliora-tion—and this healing happens only through one another, through the community in all its diversity. Embracing the challenge of this kind of healing is one of the greatest things we can offer our children. The fact remains, the spiritual marketplace is already at work on them and us—shaping attitudes and stereotypes—building walls and conceptual boxes that might otherwise sow seeds of benevolence and trust. Learning les-sons of real life, of diversity of belief, many ways to understand the basic tensions and dimensions of life, these are worthy of serious consideration in our public schools and spaces. When we get real with our kids and address these real issues, we are much more likely to engage them fully in their own learning—the intentionality of such a curriculum is clear, direct, and beneficial.

Lest we seem flippant, it is important to note the emphasis on embracing the challenge of religious diversity. Talk of diversity and religion presumes that its participants possess the fortitude to ply the trade of democracy before all else. For certain, we live in a nation governed as democratically as is practically possible (or so we like to think), a fact long established by tradition and practice. The limits of this political democra-cy are clear if we consider that we are only worthy of such governance if we continue the difficult tasks of reengaging and revisiting what it means to be democratic. This is not just a task for scholars and politicians, but must include pastors, laypersons, watchmakers, nurses, bricklayers, and teachers, to name a few. The willingness of all kinds of people to engage this tedious and trying task is essential if we are to focus on healing the wounds that scar our social landscape.

In the light of democracy, religious diversity, so often understood as an impediment to social well-being, is actually integral to a healthy and vibrant society. Diversity provides for us the opportunity to move beyond stagnation in our social processes and, as such, becomes a reservoir of greater social intelligence. As an intimate part and expression of our lives, our religious interests not only represent some of the most irreconcilable of our differences, but also some of the most irrepressible of our needs. We turn to religion when we need help, when we need a friend, and when we need comfort and assurance. There is no better well from which to draw sustenance for the challenge of reinvigorating our democracy and shaping our public schools. Given these characteristics of religion, it only makes sense to understand religious pluralism as a great opportunity for social inquiry and the advancement of democratic values. The differences that we experience here are our finest resources for healing—healing because of those very same differences, not in despite them.

To develop this idea, the healing of which we speak is ecological. The repair offered to us through religion is more than divine intervention; it is a by-product of our individual struggle to make meaning in this world, coupled with our need to enter that same struggle as it is experienced by our contemporaries. It is the progress that can only occur through the unity experienced in diversity, and *this fact* makes healing ecological (i.e., the healing occurs *because* of the diversity of our community and the cooperative inquiry necessitated by that diversity). Thus, engaging religion as a single answer robs it of its ecologically healing nature, and religious and secular orthodoxy creates a kind of poverty. As Buber said earlier, "There is no obedience to the coming one without loyalty to his creature," and such loyalty is the key to the healing function of religion. This loyalty is the heart and soul of community, it is the empathetic foundation of any genuine growth, expressed so clearly as our capacity to simply listen:

> Instead of teaching people to develop their powers of self-justification, we need to develop our capacities to hear each other, genuinely to listen to them. Listening does not mean uncritical acceptance, just as it does not mean being automatically judgmental. It is . . . a capacity to take the other's point of view into our own and through it to enlarge understanding of the situation. Only insofar as we have developed our ability to enter imaginatively into the worlds of meaning that human beings have constructed to make sense out of life, can we begin to listen to the richness of experience itself. Only then can we even begin to hear ourselves. (Alexander, 1995, p. 88)

Perhaps it sounds mundane, but the community for which Jaspers yearned and of which Buber spoke is a function of our ability to listen. The healing of which we speak is a real part of our lives and occurs *through* the struggles we are engaging every day in our schools, *through* the changes we are forced to negotiate, and *through* the diversity of religions we can encounter and engage. It is ecological and communal, and technology has created a great opportunity to use these resources. The consequence is that religious pluralism is not a problem to be overcome. Instead, it is the reservoir of greater social intelligence, the key to more effective healing. Religious pluralism *is* social inquiry because it is what best prepares us for healing, for the work of ameliorative action, but only if leaders, teachers, and mentors acknowledge their responsibility for shaping this opportunity.

Religion can be nothing other than situated in our experience. Perhaps this sounds commonplace, existing as we do in a culture insistent on experience as the sole criteria of validity,[2] but nothing could be further from the truth. The significance of this grounded, experiential understanding is to make religion much more complex, and a great deal messier, than our synagogues, sanctuaries, or mosques would lead us to believe. As we explained elsewhere, the idea that interreligious understanding must occur through commonalities between traditions and uniformity in practice is useful, but reductionistic (Carr-Chellman & Carr-Chellman, 2003). The human reality of religious experience is always more than the cultural packaging we use to contain it. Religion understood as situated in experience takes us beyond our individual boundaries. Religion understood as situated in experience, as a meaningful, purposeful human activity, is constituted with the stuff of our everyday lives. Consequently, the big, white elephant of religion is not something that can be hidden from the generations that follow us, and we create more pain, ignorance, and intolerance the bigger the elephant becomes.

PROVISIONAL PATHS
TOWARD PROVISIONAL WHOLENESS

Assuming that we refuse the modern abdication of responsibility and countenance the power of "Prometheus unbound" in the hands of our

---

[2]Throughout this chapter we refer to experience, by which we mean nothing even remotely resembling the obsessive need for experience one witnesses, for example, in the stereotypical baby-boomer lifestyle: a milquetoast and fluffy version of participation that permits and even guarantees, disengagement and superficiality. Take, for example, the emergence of seeker services designed to cater to church shoppers, whereby one's religious community must induce an experience of the divine, by which we mean that church must be entertaining. Genuine experience is not a function of ease. Instead, it is a deeply engaging event that cuts to the heart of the human ontological condition.

easily influenced children, we also accept the additional burden of engaging the constantly shifting landscape of humanity's *quest* for God—the
deeply democratic quest that challenges us to continually traverse
unknown territories in search of meaning. The precariousness of life for
which we seek to prepare our children puts us on a quest for wholeness.
The difficulty in such a quest is the constant urge to forget the *quest* for
wholeness through the fixing of wholeness itself; we yearn so much for
God, for wholeness, that we neglect the path that will let us approach that
wholeness. This is where the guardians of orthodoxy become stuck, imag-
ining that the journey is clear and the goal predetermined. But religion
understood as situated in experience—religion understood as healing—is
never fixed, never frozen in time or place; it must be constantly engaged
in the work of meeting us where we are and getting us through the day.
Religion that gets us through the day, religion that meets us where we are
and makes us better, is not, then, religion that battles for who has the
most powerful God, the most logical theology, or the brightest packaging.
Rather, it is the religion that affords us the greatest opportunity for growth:
this is the religion, "the power that can reach into the petty strivings of
plain human existence and set them aright if only provisionally"
(Anderson, 1999, p. 87). It sets our strivings aright provisionally (i.e.,
things *will* get mucked up again regardless of who or what our God is or
does). This is what it means to be engaged in the quest for wholeness, but
not the fixing of the wholeness. The following paraphrases a famous quote
from John Dewey (1939).

One way beyond the fixing of wholeness is the notion of ecology. The
complexity of a problematic situation is better discerned through a variety
of participants. Consequently, a situation in need of healing can best be
ameliorated by the greater reservoir of social intelligence contained within
a culturally and religiously diverse population. The strength of an ecosys-
tem is a function of its genetic diversity; a social system is no different: Its
ability to heal, its ability to absorb the pain of life's fluctuations, and its ability to be ameliorative are all a function of the depth of its diversity and its
willingness to engage that diversity. In this way, our social ecology—the
ontological state of an openly diverse group—becomes a kind of social
inquiry. Simply by existing ecologically, using the resources at hand (i.e.,
each other) to improve our situations, our ontological status becomes social
inquiry: the scientific method, the method of intelligence, at work. Perhaps
in this light, the importance of listening mentioned earlier becomes clearer. Again most political and social theorists and, even more, most religious
leaders and theologians look at diversity, especially religious diversity, as a
problem to be overcome. In actuality, it is our greatest hope for a healthier
world. But simple diversity is not enough. East and West must share a horizon for a new day to dawn, and disparate voices must share a language,

figuratively, for understanding to occur: Diversity is nothing without communication. Individualistic, atomistic diversity, as enticing as it is, is a kind of bondage. In such a conception of community, we remain restrained by the limitations of our own perspective. Genuine community, in contrast, is the key to a *concrete* sense of meaning in our lives. Diversity is integral to such community.

> Communities, then, are primarily groups of people who can communicate with each other. Communication, however, is not even primarily transference of information. Nor is the ultimate objective necessarily mutual agreement. . . . Communication itself is more inclusive and rich. It is the open space, the event, created by languages (verbal and non-verbal) whereby humans can share experiences and be with each other in a meaningful way. (Alexander, 1995, p. 82)

As we are only too aware, this sort of communication is not a given occurrence. The absence of our ability to hear each other across cultures and societies, to communicate and share experiences in a meaningful way, is lugubriously evident in the tragic events of September 11, of course. But, more subtly, it is also evident in the gluttonous manifestations of individuality that pervade our everyday lives. Nothing gives truth to the power of the healing properties of a religiously diverse and genuine community more clearly than the negative products of those that are not. For example, we are a nation of *individuals*, and the vision created by understanding that term independent of a diverse community is nothing short of apocalyptic.

The Founding Fathers of the United States had a very strong notion of individuality, but it leaves us searching for more when trying to engage religious diversity in a positive, growth-oriented manner. We read in Federalist Papers Number 10 and Numbers 48–52 the Madisonian argument for diversity: It was, in fact, a means to an end. If the national republic was to ever succeed, if a democracy interested in preserving the freedom of the individual above all else was to ever take steps beyond its baby crawl, James Madison argued that a diversity of conflicting interests would have to serve to prevent a large and powerful majority block from forming to suppress all dissenting voices. Part of the genius of the new republic, we remember from our eighth-grade civics class, would be the appropriate distribution of power that would serve to provide certain checks and balances, according to which one power would always oppose another. In this way, diversity was the means to the end of securing the freedom that the enlightened world so desired. This freedom was, of course, the freedom of each individual to his or her own pursuit of happiness—a negative freedom guaranteeing that no one would have enough power to infringe on my sense of individuality or my individual expression of deeply held beliefs, ethical, moral, or otherwise.

The pluralism that we struggle to achieve is for Madison only tangential to the needs of the republic. It is, in the words of Alexander (1995), "a vice that can be turned, in spite of itself, into a virtue" (p. 83). Diversity is allowed not because of the inherent good that springs from the recognition of such differences; rather it was encouraged because such diversity was irrelevant to one's citizenship. If we are to take religious diversity seriously, it must be understood as more than tangential; it must be given the weight it deserves by becoming *integral* to our understanding of the democratic process and the ameliorative approach to social ills.

We must take seriously the contributions made by our social context. In other words, we must recognize the importance of social relations and associations in the formation of who and what we are. Part and parcel of this recognition is appreciating the vital interplay of communication among and between irreconcilable differences. For example, engaging differences of religion in schools has long been completely taboo and, some would suggest, unconstitutional. Few of us could say we have never had the experience of interpersonal banter gone bad when someone or other pressed the issue of abortion, homosexuality, or salvation a bit too hard. These conversations usually do not happen in the school yard or the classroom. Sometimes they happen at family reunions, and often they happen on 24 hour news shows. These differences are among the most irreconcilable; they are what create in us the most passion and, consequently, the most frustration when someone disagrees. We do not have to accept or even like the way the world looks from this or that other perspective, "but if we are to communicate with them, we must understand how the world appears to them, for it very much constitutes *who they are*" (Alexander, 1995, p. 84; italics in original). It is precisely these issues and differences that are most important for us to embrace.

The embrace of diversity is not just about respecting who or what someone else is; even more, that embrace is about learning who *we* are in relation to that person who is so existentially different. If we are concerned about progress, if we are concerned about ameliorating the animosity that exists between, for example, the evangelical Christian and the Unitarian Universalist or between the Muslim fundamentalist and the Transcendental Meditationist, then we need to take this notion of religious pluralism as social inquiry very seriously. Understood in this way, truly our religious differences become a well of resources for social well being that will never run dry. Understood in this way, our most irreconcilable differences become integral to the proper functioning of a healthy democracy. Our diversity is a deep reservoir of greater social intelligence.

PROMETHEUS UNBOUND

Our current cultural scene is a picture of access to put Prometheus to shame, and the burden on educators to shape the use of these accessible resources is tremendous. The evidence that such access is prevalent in the realm of religion is clear. A simple search for *religion* on Google produces more than 30 million sites, *Christian* 44 million, *Christianity* 5 1/2 million, *Islam* 5 million, *Judaism*, 12 million, *Muslim* 5 million, and so forth. The information is out there. We cannot keep our children from learning that there are many ways of understanding the world, our creation, our mortality, or our immortality. Technology represents a portal through which religion can and does easily flow into our classrooms and into the lives of young, impressionable minds.

One way to guarantee that religious intolerance thrives is to ignore this situation, much like Zeus chose to ignore human progress. Another approach is to name the big, white elephant enriching our democracy with an understanding of the core values that are most sensitive and closest to our respective identities. Fine (1995), in her ethnographic examination of values education in public schools, made the link between values education and democracy most clearly:

> For democracy to work, citizens need to be able to understand and evaluate a broad range of beliefs and ideas, and to act on what they themselves believe. And that is why critical moral education is education for democracy—something we cannot do without. (p. 23)

Likewise, Moffet's (1994) text on spirituality in public schools today, *The Universal Schoolhouse,* made the case for the importance of engaging spirituality as a critical part of learning and education:

> In an age of democracy, and in the spirit of total inclusion itself, the time has come to declassify mysteries, to erase the boundaries between esoteric and exoteric. Knowledge without spirituality remains as dangerous as ever, but the worst has already been largely realized, and we now have more to lose than gain by this sort of censoring. . . . In blandly posting "the pursuit of happiness" as the American dream, even the founding fathers seem to have withheld from their general constituency (a) deeper spiritual understanding . . . both society and individuals suffer greatly if they construe personal freedom as merely material pursuit of happiness instead of as spiritual quest. (pp. 29–30)

But what we propose here is something deeper than mere inclusion. We suggest that, as a result of the ubiquitous nature of technology in schools and the weakening of traditional public institutions such as schools and traditional religious institutions, the boundaries between these systems are becoming increasingly permeable. This openness allows for a lot of different possible ways in which religion and spirituality can enter into the classroom. Spirituality can enter into our curricula as a bland topic of comparative religion in which information dispensation becomes the safe way to engage the topic. Or technology can open the boundaries of the classroom and create extreme relativism. What we suggest here, instead, is the true engagement of religion for the purposes of understanding diverse populations and the many ways of understanding our human experience as a form of ecological healing.

REFERENCES

Alexander, T. M. (1995). Educating the democratic heart: Pluralism, traditions, and the humanities. In J. Garrison (Ed.), *The new scholarship on Dewey* (pp. 75–91). Dordrecht, The Netherlands: Kluwer Academic Publishers.

Anderson, D. R. (1999). Theology as healing: A meditation on *A Common Faith*. In C. Haskins & D. Seiple (Ed.), *Dewey reconfigured: Essays on Deweyan pragmatism* (pp. 85–95). Albany: State University of New York Press.

Buber, M. (1947). *Between man and man*. London: Routledge & Kegan Paul.

Caputo, J. D. (2001). *On religion*. London: Routledge.

Carr-Chellman, D. J., & Carr-Chellman, A. A. (2003). The ecology of healing: Religious pluralism as social inquiry. In E. Farmer, J. Rojewski, & B. Farmer (Eds.), *Diversity in America: Visions of the future* (pp. 207-224. Dubuque, IA: Kendall/Hunt.

Cotton, K. (1993). *Fostering intercultural harmony in schools: Research findings*. Portland, OR: Northwest Regional Educational Laboratory.

Dewey, J. (1939). The individual in cultural crisis. In J. Ratner (Ed.), *Intelligence in the modern world: John Dewey's philosophy* (pp. 463-464). New York: Random House.

Eck, D. (2001). *A new religious America*. New York: HarperCollins.

Fine, M. (1995). *Habits of mind: Struggling over values in America's classrooms*. San Francisco: Jossey Bass.

Jaspers, K. (1957). *Man in the modern age*. New York: Anchor.

Moffett, J. (1994). *The universal schoolhouse: Spiritual awakening through education*. San Francisco: Jossey Bass.

Stuhr, J. J. (2000). Introduction to John Dewey. In J. J. Stuhr (Ed.), *Pragmatism and classical American philosophy* (pp. 431–443). Oxford: Oxford University Press.

4

CULTURE, INTERNET TECHNOLOGY, AND EDUCATION IN NORTH AMERICA AND BHUTAN

A Media Ecology Perspective

Ellen Rose

Editor's note: The Internet as a space for communication and storage provides an environment for accessing resources on many cultures, creating a virtual space for the expression of diverse voices and histories that were not heard before. This chapter invites the reader to scrutinize the biases of media and technology, placing them in an ecological relationship to culture and education. We are asked to consider the analysis of the biases of media and technology products in their control of cultural and social perceptions as being real, truthful, and inclusive.

The relation of the second media age to multiculturalism is likely, then, to be profoundly ambivalent. . . . As these technologies emerge in social space the great political question will be what forms of cultural articulation they promote and discourage. One needs to keep in mind the enormous variability of the technology rather than assume its determining powers.

—Mark Poster (2001)

In using other cultures as mirrors in which we may see our own culture
we are affected by the astigma of our own eyesight and the defects of that
mirror, with the result that we are apt to see nothing in other cultures but
the virtues of our own.

—Harold Innis (1951)

In North America, where the socioeconomic survival of individuals and organizations entails accepting cultural diversity, multiculturalism has become an ethical norm. In simple terms, it has become a moral imperative that we acknowledge and value the voices of the various peoples who make up our pluralistic society while condemning as unethical those who seek to exclude or, conversely, claim the superiority of a particular social, ethnic, or cultural group.

In recent years, through the power of "language games" (Lyotard, 1989), which it is beyond the scope of this chapter to elaborate, the discourse of the Internet has become thoroughly enmeshed within the ethic of multiculturalism. Rather ironically—because it is, after all, largely the creation of White, English-speaking males (Damarin, 1998)—the Web is increasingly represented as the online repository of resources from many cultures and the technological means by which all cultural groups, even "previously silenced voices," can "now be raised and heard" (Cummins & Sayers, 1997, p. 5). Moreover, the rhetoric surrounding the Internet further suggests that, online, skin color, ethnicity, religion, and gender are secondary to the human desire to communicate with others who share common interests. "The computer," writes one commentator, "renders [users] peculiarly colorblind. . . . Everyone comes to the conversation with a kind of equality" (Lyles, 1998, p. 114). We are led to believe that, online, the differences among people do not foment discord, but provide the basis for a diverse, rich cyberculture characterized by tolerance and respect. For instance, Negroponte (1995) enthused about the potential of digital technology to "be a natural force drawing people into greater world harmony" (p. 230), while Lévy (2001) described a cyberspace that "expresses human diversity. . . . Indeed, the multiplicity and radical integration of epochs, viewpoints, and legitimacies—the distinctive characteristic of the postmodern—are clearly accentuated and encouraged in cyberculture" (p. 101).

Given the popular conception of the online world as a democratic space that provides equal opportunities for access to information and social participation by people from diverse social, ethnic, and cultural backgrounds, access to Internet technology is increasingly represented and demanded as a fundamental right—hence, its growing presence in North American schools, where it is regarded by many as the best tool for providing students with the ability to negotiate our society's linguistic and cultural differences, and thus to become good citizens of the global village.

Travel, now, to the small kingdom of Bhutan, nestled in the Himalayan mountains between India and China, where ideas about multiculturalism and the Internet are vastly different. To the Bhutanese, the Internet represents not a means of fostering awareness and acceptance of cultural diversity, but, quite the opposite, the means by which a single, homogeneous Bhutanese culture may be represented and preserved. As the *Information Technology Master Plan for Bhutan* put it:

> Bhutan is convinced beyond the slightest doubt that IT will not only help in further development of the country by benefiting all sectors of the society, but will also be instrumental in consolidating our unique Bhutanese efforts in preserving our tradition and culture, national heritage, environment, and all that we hold dear. (Division of Information Technology, 2001, p. 26)

As Bhutan now wires its offices and classrooms, it is with the intent not of promoting diversity but of inscribing a monoculture within the nodes and networks of the World Wide Web.

The purpose of this chapter is to use the Bhutanese experience as a means of exploring, recontextualizing, and problematizing the interrelationship of culture, global information technology, and education—a complex relationship that, as Hlynka (2003) observed, has been only minimally examined. The theoretical framework in which this analysis is grounded is media ecology—a field of inquiry into human communications that has evolved from the work of such important figures as Lewis Mumford, Jacques Ellul, Harold Innis, Marshall McLuhan, and Neil Postman.

Media ecology is, of course, a product of the Western world. It arose as a means of formulating conceptual paradigms with which to study the mutual impacts of new media and the cultures into which they were introduced. Nevertheless, as a theoretical framework, media ecology is undoubtedly applicable to the Bhutanese situation. One of the primary tenets of media ecology is that "[t]echnological change is neither additive nor subtractive. It is 'ecological' in the same sense as the word is used by environmental scientists. One significant change generates total change" (Postman, 1992, p. 18). An agrarian, insular nation's attempts to import information communication technology that originated in a disparate social milieu has clear ecological implications. As Bowers (1988) pointed out, "the introduction of a technology, any technology, represents an experiment with the culture into which it is introduced" (pp. 121–122) because it is simply impossible to anticipate the impact on traditional patterns and values, or on the cultural ecology as a whole. This ecological view of communications technology will be used to shed new light not only on the cultural significance of introducing digital communication networks into Bhutanese schools and society, but also, and more important for our purposes, on the meaning of the same media when used to deliver multicultural education in the "developed"[1] world.

The first section of this chapter describes the Bhutanese perspective on Internet technology, including the political and social contexts for the kingdom's seemingly paradoxical decision to go online and introduce information technology into its educational system. The second section introduces the primary tenets of media ecology. In the third section, I undertake a media ecology analysis of the relationship between culture and the Internet informed by the disparity between the North American and Bhutanese media environments, and I conclude by proposing a new conception of multicultural education.

THE BHUTANESE CONTEXT AND PERSPECTIVE ON INTERNET TECHNOLOGY

Bhutan is a small nation ruled by a hereditary monarch, King Jigme Singye Wangchuck. The country is largely agrarian, with approximately 85% of Bhutanese people living in rural villages, many of which are unreached by telephone lines and electricity, let alone by roads. In fact until the 1960s, the lives of many Bhutanese did not differ greatly from those of their ancestors who lived in the mid-1500s (Priesner, 1999).

Since then, however, the Bhutanese government has undertaken a policy of modernization that has entailed, in particular, vast and fairly rapid improvements in the country's health and educational systems. (The latter, in particular, has undergone significant changes since the 1960s, when all education took place in the nation's monasteries. Most communities now have schools, and the attendance rate is on the rise, although it is still the case that most Bhutanese citizens are illiterate.) The concept and catch phrase guiding development in Bhutan is *Gross National Happiness*, a term coined by King Wangchuck to express long-standing cultural values and

---

[1] I place the word *developed* in scare quotes because the use of the term as a means of differentiating the nations of the world emerges from an assumption that Bhutan, as it proceeds with its plans for modernization, certainly questions: the notion that technological advancement represents the pinnacle of civilization and that, as nations adopt new technologies, they will inevitably develop social structures and values identical to those in technologically advanced (or developed) nations. Technological achievement is only one means of assessing the level of culture and civilization a nation has reached; Bhutan's state-legislated goal of Gross National Happiness is another.

beliefs derived from Buddhism (Priesner, 1999). Briefly, Gross National Happiness is based on the notion that ensuring the emotional and spiritual well-being of individual citizens is a goal more worthy than mere economic gain (as the king has put it, "Gross National Happiness is more important than Gross National Product") and the realization that the two do not always go hand in hand. As defined by Priesner (1999), Gross National Happiness suggests that:

> the overarching goal of every aspect of life, including economics, is not seen in the multiplication of material wants, which can be satisfied by consumption, but in the purification of the human character. The objectives of market economics, i.e., increasing consumption and accelerating growth are thus only relevant as means to an entirely different end—human well-being. (pp. 36–37)

One of the most important elements of Gross National Happiness is the preservation of Bhutan's unique cultural heritage. Situated as it is between two huge nations with imperialist tendencies, Bhutan has always been extremely protective of its unique culture and national identity. In implementing its policy of modernization, the government is concerned with maintaining the balance not only between growth and well-being, but also between tradition and modernity. The stated goal is to implement "change in continuity" (Mathou, 2000)—that is, change on Bhutan's own terms, in ways that accord with rather than disrupt its traditions.

Bhutan is a multi-ethnic nation. Most of the approximately 750,000 Bhutanese belong to three main ethnic communities. The Ngalongs of northwestern Bhutan comprise 15% to 20% of the population, the Sharchops of northeastern Bhutan comprise 40% to 45%, and the Nepalis in the south—most of whom are descended from Indian immigrants brought in from the 1880s on to clear forests and cultivate land in the inhospitable southern climate—represent another 40% to 50% of the population. Unlike the Hindu Nepalis, the Ngalongs and the Sharchops share a common religion, Buddhism, and have become largely integrated through intermarriage (Parmanand, 1992).

However, although it is multi-ethnic, Bhutan cannot be said to be multicultural. Indeed, according to Aris (1994), far from implying diversity, the word "'[c]ulture' tends to be conceived by the state largely in terms of those elements deliberately selected by it for the purpose of constructing a single national 'identity'" (p. 17). Centuries of defending itself against both external aggression and internal strife have resulted in the belief that national strength and survival, as well as successful modernization, depend on the maintenance of a unified, "post-ethnic" (Mathou, 2000, p. 245) Bhutanese identity based on the values, beliefs, and practices of the

Ngalong ethnic group. Most of Bhutan's governing elite, known as Drukpas, are Ngalongs; very little power is vested in members of the Nepali Bhutanese ethnic group. Thus, what the government's cultural protectiveness means in practice is that Bhutan is concerned with protecting the Ngalong culture and maintaining the cultural dominance of the Drukpas.

During the 1950s, as more and more Nepalis were recruited and welcomed into Bhutan as laborers, protecting the Drukpa culture came to mean successfully integrating the Nepali community into Bhutanese society. Nepali Bhutanese were trained for the police, army, and civil service, and Nepali–Drukpa intermarriage was promoted with cash incentives. Despite these efforts, however, the Nepalis persisted in identifying themselves with India (Sinha, 1991). They began to organize politically and to otherwise actively resist what they regarded as "a 'Bhutanisation' process whose only purpose was to favor the culturally and politically dominant group" (Mathou, 2000, p. 245). By the 1980s, Nepali political activism and demands for a democratic say in the affairs of the country meant that Bhutan had become "a scenario of escalating concern over the failure to integrate [the Nepali] portion of the population into the politically dominant Drukpa culture" (Thronson, n.d.). This concern was exacerbated by the government's conviction that there was a massive influx of illegal Nepali immigrants coming in through the country's porous southern border. By the mid-1980s, the policy of integration and assimilation had begun to give way to one of exclusion, as a result of which "more discriminatory measures were introduced, aimed at shaping a new national identity known as Drukpa" (Bureau of Democracy, Human Rights, and Labor, 2002). The government issued a "One Nation, One People" policy intended to create a distinct national identity that did not include the cultural heritage and values of the Nepali Bhutanese. Among other things, the policy stipulated that Dzongkha, Bhutan's national language, be promoted while Nepali-language education be discontinued; and that a stringent code of social etiquette and dress called *Driglam Namsha* be enforced throughout the country. Bhutanese people were now required to wear national dress— the knee-length *gho* for men and the ankle-length *kira* for women—and those who persisted in wearing Nepali dress were subject to severe fines.

In 1985, the government revised its Nationality Act to make the standards for citizenship much more rigorous. Then, in 1988, it undertook a census of southern Bhutan based on the updated act. The purpose of the census was not to gather population data, but to determine who did and did not meet the stringent new standards for citizenship. To prove their Bhutanese citizenship, the Nepalis were required to produce documentary evidence, such as tax receipts, exactly for the year 1958—even a receipt from the year before would not do. As Thronson pointed out, such a requirement would be difficult to fulfill even in "a modernized society where paper-trails are a more pervasive part of life," but for many southern Bhutanese it was simply impossible to produce the required documentation. Thus, the census and the "One Nation, One People" policy transformed thousands of people, many of whom had lived in Bhutan most or all of their life, into illegal residents whom the government proceeded to deport. The mass protests of the Nepalis throughout southern Bhutan were countered by a massive government crackdown in which thousands of protesters were arrested and detained without trial. In the ensuing violence, many Nepalis fled over the border into neighboring India, where, now homeless, they gathered in refugee camps. (It is estimated that approximately 100,000 homeless Nepalis continue to live in refugee camps near the southern border of Bhutan.) The exodus peaked in 1992, when the government instituted a campaign of systematic expulsion that involved compelling Nepalis, under threat of fine or imprisonment, to sign "voluntary" emigration papers. Eventually, having expelled approximately one third of the Nepali Bhutanese population, the government ceased its campaign, although it continues to maintain very strict control of immigration and even tourism.

This is the context for the Bhutanese government's startling decision not only to connect Bhutan via Internet to the world, but to work toward eventually providing all of the nation's schools—and, ultimately, all of its citizens—with computer and Internet access. A nation that is extremely protective of its traditional culture, and that has a history of clamping down on any forces that threaten its unity from within, has paradoxically thrown its borders wide open to the forces of globalization. In fact the initial plan was to maintain Bhutan's insularity by creating a national *intra*net that would only provide e-mail contact with the outside world, "a hermetically sealed communications system that would keep the rest of the world at bay" (Schell, 2002). However, the government was confident that, with measures of cultural preservation in place and ethnic tensions more or less resolved to its satisfaction, the country would be able to assimilate the new technology (as it once attempted to assimilate the Nepalis) on its own terms—to, as the official Kingdom of Bhutan Web page (http://www.king-domofbhutan.com/travel/travel_.html) puts it, "embrace the future and envelop it into the Bhutanese way." Indeed it was believed that the Internet could actually be used to further the goal of cultural homogeneity by "bringing together the various geographical regions and social groups in the country" (Pradhan, 2001, p. 18).

The upshot of this faith in the ability of the Internet to further the cause of a Bhutanese monoculture was that, on June 2, 1999, as part of the silver jubilee of King Wangchuck's inauguration, Druknet, Bhutan's Internet service provider, was born. Soon after, the Department of Education put forward its ambitious plan to introduce information technology (IT) into all of the country's schools within a decade and to ensure that all students were computer literate when they graduated from high school. Implementation of this plan is still in the very early stages. Although "ICT is recognized as a revolutionary industry that will benefit the education sector tremendously," it is also the case that, at this point, "[m]ost of the children in Bhutan have not even seen a computer" (Pradhan, 2001, pp. 40–41). Indeed as of September 2001, there were no computer courses in the schools and only 211 computers in the whole education sector (Pradhan, 2001).

In summary, the Bhutanese context presents an extreme contrast with contemporary North American conditions, as well as with our notions about the interrelationship of the Internet, cultural diversity, and education. Whereas North Americans tend to regard global communications networks as promoting the values of their postmodern, pluralistic society within the classroom, the Bhutanese view the same technology as a tool for fostering ethnic homogeneity. The presence of Internet technology in Bhutanese classrooms is regarded as vital not to create a culturally inclusive learning environment through access to multicultural educational resources, but for quite the opposite reason. The development of computer skills in its own people will allow the nation to produce software and Web content specifically tailored to Bhutanese needs, as identified by the dominant culture, and—an equally important factor—will allow it to do so without the necessity of importing technicians from India and other countries. In other words, the technology will enhance Bhutan's cultural homogeneity and insularity.

Well versed as they are in the ethic of multiculturalism and the rhetoric of empowerment and diversity that surrounds the Internet, most North Americans will likely have serious misgivings about both the validity and feasibility of the Bhutanese view of the message of global information media. Nevertheless, at the very least, this insight into the disparate meanings the medium assumes in different societies provides the basis for problematizing and recontextualizing assumptions about multicultural education via the Internet that prevail in the technologically developed world. Media ecology provides a useful lens through which we can further examine both the North American and Bhutanese perspectives.

THE PRIMARY TENETS OF MEDIA ECOLOGY

The key idea that unites the diverse works of media ecologists such as Mumford, Ellul, Innis, McLuhan, and Postman is that technologies are not simply neutral artifacts, but are, rather, the embodiment of ideas, values, assumptions, procedures, and modes of organization. This idea is perhaps most succinctly expressed in McLuhan's well-known but little understood aphorism, "the medium is the message." In *The End of Education*, Postman (1995), elaborated on this first principle of media ecology:

Embedded in every technology there is a powerful idea, sometimes two or three powerful ideas. Like language itself, a technology predisposes us to favor and value certain perspectives and accomplishments and to subordinate others. Every technology has a philosophy, which is given expression in how the technology makes people use their minds, in what it makes us do with our bodies, in how it codifies the world, in which of our senses it amplifies, in which of our emotional and intellectual tendencies it disregards. (p. 192)

Likewise, according to Innis (1951), structures of communication contain built-in biases, such that societies like Bhutan's, in which the primary medium is spoken language, value continuity, practical knowledge, immediate experience, and local tradition, whereas societies such as ours, in which distance-bridging technologies such as TV and the Internet prevail, accord a much higher value to linear and abstract thought.

Far from being neutral, then, media promote transformations, often radical, in social values and ultimately in societies and the institutions—governments, economies, educational systems—of which they are comprised. The notion that media embody ideas and wreak social, cultural, and even psychological change is in sharp contrast to the typical conceptualization of media as neutral conduits through which we send information, of which the Shannon and Weaver (1949) model is perhaps the best-known example. In education, assertions regarding the neutrality of media take the form of the common claim that IT is "only a tool" (Robertson, 2001; Rose, 2002) whose biases and effects need not be examined, an unquestioned premise that has provided the imprimatur for a focus, in the discourse of computer-based instruction, largely on the content that the purportedly neutral tool is used to deliver.

Related to this first tenet of media ecology is the notion that, far from constituting mere neutral pipelines, our modes of communication form in their totality an *environment* that surrounds us as completely and, as McLuhan often observed, as invisibly as air. In Ellul's (1980) words, technology "is the engulfing element, inside of which everything is situated" (p. 194). Postman (1979) concurred:

Every society is held together by certain modes and patterns of communication which control the kind of society it is. One may call them information systems, codes, message networks, or media of communication. Taken together they set and maintain the parameters of thought and learning within a culture. Just as the physical environment determines what the source of food and exertions of labor shall be, the information environment gives specific direction to the kinds of ideas, social attitudes, definitions of knowledge, and intellectual capacities that will emerge. (p. 29)

A corollary of this second principle is that the introduction of a new medium into the information environment will always have ecological implications. That is to say, it will upset the existing sociocultural balance. When rabbits were introduced into the Australian outback in the mid-19th century, the result was not the same environment plus rabbits, but a whole new environment in which the ecological balance and conditions of survival had been dramatically altered. In the same way, 50 years after the printing press was introduced into medieval society, the result was not "old Europe plus the printing press," but "a very different Europe" (Postman, 1992, p. 18), in which habits of mind and social relationships had been radically transformed by the biases (linearity, repeatability, uniformity) of print.

However, just as in the natural world, such changes are never predictable (Postman, 1982), but depend in large part on the "cultural matrix within which the particular medium operates" (McLuhan, 1964, p. 11). The "biases" of rabbits may be to procreate rapidly and decimate low-growing vegetation, but rabbits doubtless play a different role in the Arctic environment than they do in Australia. Similarly, in the ecology of media, the effect of a medium is determined not only by its inherent biases, but also by its interactions within "a complex web of interrelationships among society, culture, and individuals" (Barnes & Strate, 1996, p. 183). Mumford (1934) took this notion of the mutual determinations of technology and human culture as his theme in *Technics and Civilization*. He contended that the connection between a technology and the culture in which it exists is so vital that it is futile to examine the former in isolation from a consideration of the latter: "The machine cannot be divorced from its larger social pattern; for it is this pattern that gives it meaning and purpose" (p. 110).

A final point on which media ecologists tend to agree has to do with the absolute importance of achieving awareness of our media environment because a clear-sighted, critical contemplation is, in their view, the only means by which we can avoid being overrun by technology and thus maintain a healthy ecological balance. However, media ecologists are also in agreement about the difficulty of achieving this important goal because as media become part of the fabric of everyday life, they become increasingly invisible to us. As McLuhan and Fiore (1968) put it, "One thing about which fish know exactly nothing is water" (p. 175). Exploring the different ways in which digital communications networks come to bear in different societies—for instance, the small Himalayan kingdom of Bhutan—is one strategy for making strange and thus visible our own media environment. Another is education: Media ecologists share a belief in the importance of education (Barnes & Strate, 1996) and, in particular, the necessity of reconceptualizing education as the means by which students can achieve an understanding of and epistemological distance from their media environment. We must, contended Ellul (1981), teach our children "to live *in* technology" while also helping them "to develop a critical awareness of the modern world" (p. 83).

In summary, media ecology begins with the premise that media contain inherent biases that transform societies and cultures. However, the determinism of this initial premise is considerably softened—first by the notion that the relationship between media and culture is ecological and thus mutually determining, and, second, by the belief that media effects can be mitigated by an education that teaches students to see and think critically about their information environment.

A MEDIA ECOLOGY ANALYSIS

Having briefly described the fundamental principles of media ecology, I now use them as the basis for an analysis of the interrelationship of culture, education, and Internet technology in the context of both North American and Bhutanese media environments.

A media ecology perspective on the instructional use of the Internet contrasts sharply with many discussions on the subject, which reflect the belief that what is important is the cultural diversity of the content being delivered by the Internet while the medium is represented as a neutral pipeline connecting disparate peoples and culturally inclusive resources. Thus, texts on the potential of the Internet for promoting multicultural awareness tend to dwell on content-related issues such as cultural representations, the incorporation of multiple viewpoints and perspectives, and the analysis of the underlying ideologies of media artifacts. Important as such considerations are, content is only one aspect of multicultural education. It is, however, the dimension that is the most "easily realized through technology" (Marshall, 2001). Indeed the biases of the Internet and its search engines are such that the concern with content tends to devolve into the mere identification of online multicultural resources (e.g., Beck, 2002; Gorski, 2000; Gregory, Stauffer, & Keene, 1999), as if simply having access to diverse curricular materials and opportunities for e-mail exchanges with students from other countries constitute adequate concession to the ethical demands of multiculturalism. Engrossed as we are with the content displayed on Web pages and the practical uses of the "tool" for accessing and delivering that content, by and large we neglect to consider the important roles that the Internet, and the social and political interests and structures that support it, play in shaping cultural values and mores, including the way in which the content is received and used.

A similar attitude toward global information networks appears to prevail in Bhutan, where reports and other texts about the introduction of IT tend to represent the new media strictly as delivery mechanisms for Bhutanese content. Hence, the concern expressed in the *Information Technology Master Plan* with digitizing important Bhutanese religious texts and working with application manufacturers to develop a software plug-in that will translate the menus and commands of the Windows operating system into Dzongkha (Division of Information Technology, 2001). Underlying all such plans is the belief that what is important is the cultural specificity of the content being delivered by the Internet while the medium is represented as fundamentally neutral.

What media ecology brings to this discussion, then, is the understanding that the content transmitted by a medium is less significant and, ultimately, has less effect on a society or culture than the medium itself. In McLuhan's (1964) terms, "the 'content' of a medium is like the juicy piece of meat carried by the burglar to distract the watchdog of the mind" (p. 26) from asking questions about the inherent biases of a technology and the way it comes to bear within a particular culture.

What, then, are the biases of the Internet? In *The Bias of Communication*, Innis (1951) asserted that one of the foremost proclivities of high-tech modes of communication is the extension of social control over vast areas of space. In the discourse of the Internet, this tendency is celebrated as the ability of digital communication networks to annihilate geographical distance—to bring people together into a global embrace. Indeed the assertion that distance has been rendered irrelevant has been made so many times—beginning, perhaps, with McLuhan's (1962) description of how the simultaneity and interdependence of electric media such as the telegraph and radio shrink the planet to a single "global village" (p. 31)—that it no longer requires saying. The now-familiar image of a globe criss-crossed by a web has become visual shorthand for the abolishment of geographical distance: We are meant to see not a vast and mysterious planet, but a well-defined, knowable sphere contained within a single, all-encompassing Net. A recent Rogers AT&T advertisement for cell phones pairs this image with the caption, "Who really cares about geography anymore?" No one, it would seem, needs to because as human interactions move online, they are said to become "decoupled from geography" (Negroponte, 1995, p. 166) or "deterritorialized" (Lévy, 2001, p. 186). Because any node in the Net can now connect instantly with any other node, business people can conduct transactions with people and organizations on the other side of the globe without ever leaving their offices. As for education, we are repeatedly assured that, in a world in which students everywhere can access global content and interact as a virtual class, the distinction between online and onsite education is rendered increasingly irrelevant. Indeed in the discourse of educational technology, distance seems to be falling not only out of vogue, but out of our vocabulary and thought world, to be replaced by talk of access, communication, accommodation, connectivity, and "open," "flexible," or just plain "e" learning. In the world in general, and in the realm of education in particular, it would seem that, as Cairncross (1997) boldly asserted, distance is well and truly "dead."

The current North American concern with fostering multiculturalism in the classroom is clearly related to the overwhelming sense that geography no longer matters. Because if we do indeed live in a global village, then it behooves us to help youngsters learn more about its other citizens. A media ecology perspective, however, suggests the limitations of this simplistic view. Indeed Innis (1951) made a cogent case for regarding modern media that annihilate distance as actually promoting not social cohesion, but its opposite: the erosion of traditional culture and community bonds. According to Innis spoken language is a "time-binding" medium, meaning that cultures in which it is the primary mode of communication are concerned with the endurance and continuity of values and traditions. Conversely, more modern technologies, from print to the Internet, are "space-binding," in the sense that the cultures in which they are dominant tend to be concerned with exercising control over space, whether through war, colonization, the global embrace of the Internet, or even attempts to reach and settle other planets. In space-bound societies such as our own, people tend to disperse as the concerns for religion and community that play such a vital role in holding oral, time-bound cultures together give way to secular, commercial interests (Innis, 1951). Similarly, a concern with concrete experience, emotion, and immediacy gives way to the privileging of abstract knowledge, rationality, and impersonal, often monetary, exchanges between remote parties.

Menzies (1997) expanded on Innis' formulation, showing how digital networks, interacting with the imperatives of a market economy, promote "telework"—computer-based work that can be performed away from central offices and production facilities—and other relations of employment that isolate people and dissolve social bonds:

> The work is de-institutionalized into commoditized modules. What had been a coherent group, if not a community, of people working in direct association with each other over time becomes a set of social isolates linked digitally and only for the life of a contract or project. (Menzies, 1999, p. 550)

Menzies (1999) also emphasized a second important bias of the Internet as it is manifested within a market economy such as our own: the acceleration of time. More and more, she wrote, people "are driven by the pace built into these networks through their accelerating processing speeds and instant global connections" (p. 551). As we are driven to keep pace with technologies that enable instantaneous communications and calculations, the clock becomes an increasingly central fact of life and the standard against which most human activity is measured in North America. "Time," wrote McLuhan (1964), "measured not by the uniqueness of private experience but by abstract uniform units gradually pervades all sense life" (p. 146). Indeed Mumford (1934) went so far as to describe the clock as "the key-machine" (p. 14) of our culture, by which he meant that the biases of the clock—a valuing of efficiency, standardization, automatic action, accuracy, and mathematical measurement, and a concomitant devaluing of the rhythms of the human body and the natural world—gave rise to and have been perpetuated in subsequent technological developments in the Western world. Thus, Mumford would assert that the Internet, with its electric speed, carries the biases of the clock into the information age, where the tempo of life is further accelerated.

Of course it is often claimed that the Internet makes clock time irrelevant: Business communications can be conducted across multiple time zones, and e-learning modules can be completed at any time of the day. Although actual clock time may indeed become less meaningful, the demands of the market economy are such that the biases of the clock—the imperatives of instantaneous speed, standardization, and machine-like efficiency—persist, with the technology often serving not only to drive people faster, but also, increasingly, to monitor and report on their accuracy and rate of performance. This is certainly true in the case of technology-based education, in which the computer functions not only as a "productivity tool," serving "to enhance efficiency and effectiveness in response to [a] problem or assignment" (Forcier, 1999, p. 34), but also as a means of tracking those aspects of student progress and achievement that are quantifiable—while rendering those factors that defy quantification irrelevant. As they demand speed and standardization of response from their human users, digital technologies promote homogeneity, because, increasingly, the standards that govern social action bear less relation to a grounded time and place than to a cyberculture dominated by the technical values of efficiency, accuracy, and quantification. In this way, the electric speed of technology works toward "the elimination of all human variability" (Ellul, 1964, p. 135) or, in McLuhan's more utopian terms, toward the mingling of all cultures in a single, global consciousness.

Thus, a media ecology perspective suggests that, when introduced into North America's market economy, the Internet will tend to create an environment in which the primary conditions of survival have to do with one's willingness to forsake local tradition while adapting to the rapid pace of cyberculture. Regardless of the content diffused on the Web, the "message" of the medium, at least insofar as it comes to bear in our society, seems to have less to do with the formation of rich cross-cultural connections than with the creation of solitary servomechanisms who function primarily as efficient processors of decontextualized information—and who paradoxically regard the medium that enforces their homogeneity and growing physical and psychological distance from each other as a means of fostering interpersonal and intercultural communications. Contrary to assumptions that the Internet will provide the basis of a diverse, tolerant online culture, a media ecology perspective suggests that the global village is, of necessity, a site of "discontinuity and division," of "spite and envy" (McLuhan & Stearn, 1967, p. 272), in which high-tech media, and inevitable struggles for media control, paradoxically curtail understanding (Innis, 1951). In short, when brought into conjunction with a capitalist ethos, what Internet technology produces is not the global village mythologized in the discourse of multiculturalism, but "globalization," an economic situation in which cultural diversity is leveled by thriving, predatory, transnational corporations:

> It might be said that what is remarkable about globalization is its capacity to erode anything genuinely remarkable, its levelling of the world into what is sometimes called McWorld. . . . Other ways of life, other social conventions and other cultural traditions are subordinated to the transnationalist world view. (Workman, 2003, p. 37)

How will the space- and time-compressing tendencies of the Internet come to bear in Bhutan? Although the complex ecological interrelationships between culture and technology are impossible to predict, a media ecology perspective suggests that we can expect the reciprocal effects of Internet technology and this rural, largely oral culture to be quite different from what we are witnessing in North America. Given that the Bhutanese are less concerned with Gross National Product than with Gross National Happiness, the tendency of the Internet to accelerate time and to compel people to accommodate their lives to the imperatives of speed and efficiency may be neutralized. As for the Internet's tendency to annihilate physical distance, it is quite possible that this bias may actually function, in Bhutan's barter economy, to reduce the psychological distances separating the cultural groups—thus, in McLuhan's terms, retribalizing Bhutanese society. In short, introduced into an environment in which there are no impinging demands for efficiency, accuracy, and standardization, in which life is governed by Buddhist tenets rather than a hyped-up version of the Protestant work ethic, the Internet may indeed become a meeting place for disparate groups, thus serving to promote social unity and cohesiveness, rather than homogenization.

What a media ecology analysis suggests, then, is that it is a mistake to regard the Internet as a neutral pipeline whose cultural significance can be regulated through control of the content it is used to disperse. On the contrary, the biases of Internet technology are such that, when introduced into these disparate environments, they may come to bear in ways that are, in both cases, fundamentally at odds with the prevailing social ethic. In North America, where the goal is to enhance inclusiveness and communications among cultural groups, the technology is tending to increase social distance and promote the creation of a homogeneous cyberculture. In Bhutan, where the goal is to cultivate a national identity or monoculture, the technology may actually foster the creation of an online commons in which various ethnic groups find opportunities to express their uniqueness.

MULTICULTURAL EDUCATION RECONCEIVED

Of course neither of these outcomes should be regarded as a *fait accompli*. The only point that a media ecologist would assert with certainty is that the emergence or wholesale introduction of a new mode of communication will inevitably disrupt the status quo, or ecological balance, of a given information environment through its power to subtly "alter those deeply embedded habits of thought which give to a culture its sense of what the world is like—a sense of what is the natural order of things, of what is reasonable, of what is necessary, of what is inevitable, of what is real" (Postman, 1992, p. 12). Moreover, it is important to keep in mind that such deterministic outcomes can always be countered by an education that functions as "civil defense against media fallout" (McLuhan, 1964, p. 305). Media ecologists agree that education is the primary means for developing a resistance to media biases, but only if it is an education aimed not at immersing students in and acclimatizing them to the media environment, but at helping them to see and scrutinize it. This means making the technology, and its ecological relationship to culture, a subject of critical analysis and discussion. Therefore, according to Postman (1995), an education informed by the precepts of media ecology

> is mainly about how television and movie cameras, Xerox machines, and computers reorder our psychic habits, our social relations, our political ideas, and our moral sensibilities. It is about how the meanings of information and education change as new technologies intrude upon a culture, how the meanings of truth, law, and intelligence differ among oral cultures, writing cultures, printing cultures, electronic cultures. (p. 191)

The hope is that the student who understands the biases of technology, and the way they work to control perceptions, can better resist such determining effects: "[O]nly through a deep and unfailing awareness of the structure and effects of information, through a demystification of media, is there any hope of our gaining some measure of control over television, or the computer, or any other medium" (Postman, 1985, p. 161), and thus of making it serve the social ends we want it to serve, whatever those ends might be.

Ultimately, a media ecology analysis suggests that, given the ecological relationship between culture and technology, multicultural education must be reconceived. Preparing students to become good citizens of the global village involves much more than a curricular or content-based response to the ethical imperative of acknowledging cultural diversity. Indeed, as long as we insist on regarding and representing the Internet as a neutral conduit through which we can distribute and access ethnically diverse content, it is likely that the kind of tolerance we seek to instill in North American students will remain a chimera. This is because the biases of the Internet, as they come to bear in our market economy, actually tend to inhibit cross-cultural understanding. Thus, as Innis (1951) predicted in the second epigraph of this chapter, we are likely to condemn as inappropriate and wrong-minded the Bhutanese view of Internet technology as a means of fostering a monoculture—even though true inclusiveness would entail an understanding of *all* cultures, even those that are emphatically not multicultural. A media ecology perspective overcomes the biases of the Internet and other modes of communication insofar as it exposes them, helping us to understand the integral relationship among behaviors, predispositions, and habits of mind (both our own and those of other peoples) and the media environment. The media are not simply neutral conduits for the dissemination of information. Rather, they play a key role in the actual construction of social and personal identities. Therefore, instilling in students a multicultural awareness necessarily entails the promotion of a media ecology perspective—that is, an understanding not only of the interdependence of people and nations, but of media and culture. Acknowledging and exploring such complex ecological interrelationships is the essence of a global education and the foundation of a truly multicultural perspective.

REFERENCES

Aris, M. (1994). Introduction. In M. Aris & M. Hutt (Eds.), *Bhutan: Aspects of culture and development* (pp. 7-23). Gartmore, Scotland: Kiscadale.

Barnes, S., & Strate, L. (1996, Fall). The educational implications of the computer: A media ecology critique. *The New Jersey Journal of Communication, 4*(2), 180–208.

Beck, P. (2002). *GlobaLinks: Resources for world studies, grades K-8.* Worthington, OH: Linworth.

Bowers, C. S. (1988). *The cultural dimensions of computing: Understanding the non-neutrality of technology.* New York: Teachers College Press.

Bureau of Democracy, Human Rights, and Labor. (2002, March). *2001 country reports on human rights practices.* Washington, DC: U.S. Department of State. Retrieved June 20, 2003, from < http://www.bhootan.org/usdept/state_dept_2001.htm >.

Cairncross, F. (1997). *The death of distance: How the communications revolution will change our lives.* Boston: Harvard Business School Press.

Cummins, J., & Sayers, D. (1997). *Brave new schools: Challenging cultural illiteracy through global learning networks.* New York: St. Martin.

Damarin, S. (1998, Winter). Technology and multicultural education: The question of convergence. *Theory Into Practice, 37*(1), 11-19.

Division of Information Technology. (2001, March). *Information technology master plan for Bhutan.* Bhutan: Ministry of Communications.

Ellul, J. (1964). *The technological society* (J. Wilkinson, Trans.). New York: Vintage Books.

Ellul, J. (1980). *The technological system* (J. Neugroschel, Trans.). New York: Continuum.

Ellul, J. (1981). *Perspectives on our age: Jacques Ellul speaks on his life and work* (W. H. Vanderburg, Ed.; J. Neugroschel, Trans.). Toronto: Canadian Broadcasting Corporation.

Forcier, R. C. (1999). *The computer as an educational tool: Productivity and problem solving* (2nd ed.). Upper Saddle River, NJ: Merrill.

Gorski, P. (2000, September). Bridges on the I-way: Multicultural resources online. *Multicultural Review, 9*(3), 68-70.

Gregory, V. L., Stauffer, M. H. K., & Keene, T. W. (1999). *Multicultural resources on the Internet: The United States and Canada.* Englewood, CO: Libraries Unlimited.

Hlynka, D. (2003, July/August). The cultural discourses of educational technology: A Canadian perspective. *Educational Technology, 43*(4), 41-45.

Innis, H. A. (1951). *The bias of communication.* Toronto: University of Toronto Press.

Lévy, P. (2001). *Cyberculture* (R. Bononno, Trans.). Minneapolis: University of Minnesota Press.

Lyles, C. (1998). CyberFaith: Promoting multiculturalism online. In R. Holeton (Ed.), *Composing cyberspace: Identity, community, and knowledge in the electronic age* (pp. 113-115). Boston: McGraw-Hill.

Lyotard, J. (1989). *The postmodern condition: A report on knowledge* (G. Bennington & B. Massumi, Trans.). Minneapolis: University of Minnesota Press.

Marshall, P. L. (2001). *Multicultural education and technology: Perfect pair or odd couple?* Retrieved July 7, 2003, from ERIC Database. (ERIC Document Reproduction Service No. ED460129.)

Mathou, T. (2000, Winter). The politics of Bhutan: Change in continuity. *Journal of Bhutan Studies, 2*(2), 228-262.

McLuhan, M. (1962). *The Gutenberg galaxy: The making of typographic man.* London: Routledge.

McLuhan, M. (1964). *Understanding media: The extensions of man.* New York: McGraw-Hill.

McLuhan, M., & Fiore, Q. (1968). *War and peace in the global village*. New York: Bantam.

McLuhan, M., & Stearn, G. E. (1967). A dialogue: Q & A. In G. E. Stearn (Ed.), *McLuhan: Hot and cool* (pp. 259-292). New York: Dial.

Menzies, H. (1997, Summer). Telework, shadow work: The privatization of work in the new digital economy. *Studies in Political Economy, 53*, 103-123.

Menzies, H. (1999). Digital networks: The medium of globalization, and the message. *Canadian Journal of Communication, 24*, 539-555.

Mumford, L. (1934). *Technics and civilization*. New York: Harcourt, Brace.

Negroponte, N. (1995). *Being digital*. New York: Vintage Books.

Parmanand. (1992). *The politics of Bhutan: Retrospect and prospect*. Delhi: Pragati Publications.

Poster, M. (2001). *Essays: The information subject*. Amsterdam: G + B Arts.

Postman, N. (1979). *Teaching as a conserving activity*. New York: Dell.

Postman, N. (1982). *The disappearance of childhood*. New York: Vintage Books.

Postman, N. (1985). *Amusing ourselves to death: Public discourse in the age of show business*. New York: Penguin.

Postman, N. (1992). *Technopoly: The surrender of culture to technology*. New York: Vintage Books.

Postman, N. (1995). *The end of education: Redefining the value of school*. New York: Alfred A. Knopf.

Pradhan, G. (2001, September). *Study of the development of ICT in the kingdom of Bhutan*. Bhutan: IDRC.

Priesner, S. (1999). Gross national happiness—Bhutan's vision of development and its challenges. In *Gross national happiness: Discussion papers* (pp. 24-52). Thimpu, Bhutan: The Centre for Bhutan Studies.

Robertson, H. J. (2001). But it's only a tool! Deconstructing the defense. In M. Moll (Ed.), *But it's only a tool! The politics of technology and education reform* (pp. 13-42). Ottawa, ON: Canadian Centre for Policy Alternatives.

Rose, E. (2002, December). Fuzzy logic: Computers, education, and language in a techno-illogical world. *Bulletin of Science, Technology and Society, 22*(6), 513-517.

Schell, O. (2002, February 13). *Gross national happiness: Bhutan meets the World Wide Web and the World Wrestling Federation*. Retrieved May 13, 2002, from < http://www.redherring.com/insider/2002/0213/1614.html > .

Shannon, C. E., & Weaver, W. (1949). *The mathematical theory of communication*. Urbana: University of Illinois Press.

Sinha, A. C. (1991). *Bhutan: Ethnic identity and national dilemma*. New Delhi: Reliance Publishing House.

Thronson, D. B. (no date). *Ethnic cleansing: Distinct national identity and the refugees from southern Bhutan*. Retrieved June 20, 2003, from < http://www.bhootan.org/thronson/thronson_intro.htm > .

Workman, T. (2003). *Social torment: Globalization in Atlantic Canada*. Halifax: Fernwood.

5

FACE TO FACE IN A THIRD SPACE

Hypertext Design and Curriculum Theory

David Shutkin

Editor's note: In this chapter, Shutkin considers the relationships forged through the use of hypertext and the recognition of the ethical, with the concept of responsibility for the other. In doing so, Shutkin argues that we need to question the reification of culture and the Western assumptions of cultural diversity. In taking this position, Shutkin challenges the notions of *truth* found in official educational texts, while making a call for the use of hypertext to open up new possibilities for recognizing the identity of the other.

Here I am thrown back toward an immemorial past.

—Emmanuel Levinas (1998a)

The great challenge of our time is to think beyond the paradox of identity and the other.

—Cameron McCarthy (1998)

In this chapter, I consider Levinas' (1985) concept of ethical responsibility of the self for the other as I question a textbook's version of the history of America's indigenous peoples. Ethical responsibility emerges as a struggle to bear witness to the responsibility for the other. Drawing on postcolonial thought, I understand culture as a performance of difference constantly interrupting linear claims that would have a singular past relate to a unique present. There is a homology, I argue, among this form of ethical responsibility, postcolonial thought, and the emerging medium of hypertext. This homology suggests strategies for reconstructing history texts in webbed environments using hypertext, a medium marked by recursion and multiplicity. Placing emphasis on an ephemeral relation of the self to the Other, these strategies are relational, situated, non-linear, and overflowing of the formal boundaries of traditional narrative and historiography.

THE REDUCTION OF THE OTHER
TO THE KNOWING SUBJECT

A course I teach on the multilinear and non-narrative form of hypertext explores hypermedia technologies including the World Wide Web. The course combines lecture and discussion in a computer classroom as it relates hypertext design to curriculum. In the context of postcolonial thought and cultural theory, hypertext is compared with documentary film, classic animation, school textbooks, and experimental fiction. As a digital medium, hypertext enables the production of links or transition points from a designated location in one document (i.e., a word, graphic image, or table) to a designated location within that same document or to a different document. A relatively new medium with uncertain and unfamiliar conventions, hypertext integrates written text with audio, video, still images, and digital effects. Hypertext is made familiar by the international computer network commonly referred to as the World Wide Web.

For a class session on the cultural politics of the textbook and possibilities for hypertext design, I arbitrarily selected a 1997 secondary textbook on the history of the United States from the university library.[1] Chapter 1 is entitled, "The First Americans" (*Beginnings to 1500*). I digitally reproduced the first page and projected it on the screen in class:

---

[1]L. Mason, W. Jacobs, & R. Ludlum (1997) *History of the United States: Beginnings to 1877*. Evanston, IL: McDougal Littell.

An early scholar who thought seriously about the origin of the Native Americans was Thomas Jefferson. . . . Where, he asked two centuries ago, did America's native people come from? Jefferson suggested that the eastern inhabitants of Asia may have passed into America across the Bering Strait. . . . But no one 200 years ago, or even 100 years ago, had the evidence to prove Jefferson right or wrong. Today scientists have proof. Studies of languages, of blood types, of teeth, of bones, even climate, all point to the answer, Jefferson was right.

For class that week, we read a chapter by Hall (1997) entitled, "The Spectacle of the 'Other.'" In that chapter, Hall introduced the concept of *regime of representation* and defined it as, ". . . the whole repertoire of [textual] imagery and visual affects through which 'difference' is represented at any one historical moment . . ." (p. 232). Class discussion focused on how this disturbing narrative forms a regime of representation. Later, discussion shifted to consider the limits of this regime and how it might be reconstructed and perhaps subverted through the integration of hypertext. To underscore its claims to truth, the textbook chapter weaves together through its narrative a multiplicity of Eurocentric discourses on Manifest Destiny, individualism, anthropology, and the veracity of Western science. As the narrative begins, the protagonist, a "serious scholar," a familiar paternal figure, Thomas Jefferson, is introduced. The story line has this hero wondering about the mysterious Other he and his comrades frequently encounter. Disclosing the discourse on Manifest Destiny and territorial expansion (which would later inform Democratic and Republican rhetoric for more than 100 years), the narrative has Jefferson question from where these peoples had come. Effectively eliding/invalidating any claim these peoples may or may not have to the Americas as indigenous or original peoples, Jefferson pondered whether this Other may have arrived to the Americas from Asia. Rising to its point of highest action, a scientific discourse, of evidence, proof, and (strangely) truth, emerges in the narrative. An anthropological discourse enters next, and the narrative finds closure as all loose ends are neatly resolved—with the tone and point of view of this chapter and textbook securely in place.

Constructed through the formation of this regime of representation and the weaving together of these discourses is the subject of chapter 1—"The First Americans." Most significant, it is through this weaving of discourses that this Native Other is constructed as the subject of this chapter. This weaving is an assimilating, appropriating, incorporating, absorbing, and transforming of the Native Other into a discursive object that can be recognized and understood by the author of this narrative—the subject of power. Across the pages of this history text, first nation peoples do not speak in their own voice. Instead this native other is presented to the reader through a narrative authorized by the subject of power (Critchley, 1992; Levinas, 1996; Peperzak, 1993).

As a discursive formation, this introductory narrative assumes that the reader is a White European male gazing on remnants of a Native Other—reduced to a fragmented epistemological corpus of "blood, teeth and bones." Through its weaving of discourses and its reliance on the conventions of narrative (coherent point of view, rising action, neatly sutured resolution, etc.), this history text follows the tradition of Western philosophy to erase the complexities of the Other not commonly understood from the dominant perspective of the White European male.

THE EXCESS OF THE OTHER

The face is present in its refusal to be contained

—Emmanuel Levinas (1998c)

Although Levinas (1996, 1998c) criticized that liberty for the subject of power is an uninhibited freedom to assimilate all otherness, it is the questioning, critiquing, and resisting by the Other of this freedom of the subject of power that Levinas refered to as the ethical. The ethical is the point of alterity, of otherness, that refuses reduction to the subject of power. Indeed Levinas (1996, 1998c) nominated the Other as excess—as the alterity that cannot be reduced to the totality of the subject of power.

This ethical concept of excess can be used productively in a digital environment to question and challenge the authority of the subject of power. As it enables the production of links from a designated location in one text to a designated location within that text, or to an altogether different text, hypertext is a digital medium that can be used to explore and represent the excesses of the Other. Even before the first assignment in my hypertext course, I have already encouraged students to appropriate this medium as a knowledge tool to subvert and/or refuse the linear structure of conventional top–down narrative, chronology and historiography. Beginning with the narrative of "The First Americans," I demonstrate how the excesses of the Other overflow the narrative boundaries of traditional history and how this might be represented through hypertext.

While students read "The First Americans," I digitally embellish the text with graphic overlays to establish the cultural politics of this Eurocentric textbook. Through these practices, I describe the formation of this text as a regime of representation, including its graphic techniques, effects, and strategies of comprehension—totalizing chronologies, hierarchies, and narratives (Hall, 1997). The first overlay is a photograph of Tom Torlino, a member of the Apache Nation subjected in the 19th century to forced assimilation at the Carlyle Indian School in Pennsylvania (Malmsheimer, 1985). His likeness is partially covered by a portrait of slave holder and third president of the United States, Thomas Jefferson, next by the insignia of the American Anthropological Association, until a montage of visual images, signifiers of the hegemony of Western science, eclipses any last remaining pixels of Tom Torlino.[2]

Annotated and linked to the narrative are the Web sites of *The Circle* (2003), a Native American journal of news and the arts, the Center for World Indigenous Studies, (2003), an international project to document the histories of the world's indigenous peoples. Links are also made to the PBS Web site, Africans in America (2003) which constructs a revisionist historiography of the states that offers significant challenges to this regime of representation. There is a link to *Rethinking Schools Online* (2003), a radical curriculum journal produced by teachers that includes a provocative special issue challenging the narrative point of view of the Discovery. I also established an internal link to translated excerpts from the memoirs of Bartolome de las Casas, a priest who journeyed with Columbus, which document the genocide perpetrated by the Spanish during their conquest of the Americas. Further links are made to the postcolonial writings of Harding (1998), relating science to colonial domination and to the critical writings of anthropologist Rosaldo (1993), which challenge the hegemony of Anthropological discourse. Suddenly, the neat and tidy narrative featuring Thomas Jefferson and first nation peoples, authored through the pages of this history text, is overwhelmed by a multiplicity of discourses vying to make known very different narrative possibilities.

FACE TO FACE IN AN IMMEMORIAL PAST

For Levinas, as I introduced, the ethical is the point of alterity that resists reduction or assimilation to the subject of power. Exceeding the limited understanding of the Other by the subject of power, the ethical is described by Levinas (1998c) as an exteriority.[3] Further, he used the neologism of the

---

[2]In one episode of Africans in America, Thomas Jefferson was described simultaneously as the author of American democracy and as a slave holder. Read directly from the archives of his estate are the names and the dollar amounts received for each of his former slaves sold to payoff his debt.

[3]This reference to the ethical no more implies the commonsense notion of an obligatory code of moral practices—a deontology, than the face of the other refers to those plastic features perceived, known and understood as "the human face."

face to refer this exteriority (Critchley, 1992). The face cannot be compre-
hended (as a material object of cognition), nor can it be seen (as a material object of perception). Instead as a relation of the self to the Other, the face
defines the ethical. This face to face, as it is commonly discussed, suggests
an unconditional responsibility for the Other that comes before the subject
directly and externally as epiphany (Levinas, 1998c).[4] The ethical face is
inconsistent with the ontological assumptions of Western discourse, which
emphasize singular truth, perception, intention, hierarchy, and domination.

Yet the face constitutes the subject of power's condition of possibility.
The subject first recognizes himself, comes into being, in this ethical face
to face. Consider the instance of Frederick Kemmelmyer's painting, First
Landing of Christopher Columbus.[5] Reproduced in the second chapter of
the 1997 secondary textbook introduced earlier, this painting represents
Columbus and his men in the foreground, the fleet behind them, and
immediately to their left a gathering of Arawak peoples. It is illustrative, if
not significant, that at the very instant considered in this painting,
Columbus' gaze has not yet turned toward the Arawak peoples. In that
instant, Columbus stands face to face with the Arawak before he actually
sees them—before his perception, intention, or domination. In just that
instant, the ethical face to face precedes the assimilation and reduction of
the Other.

This face to face is a Saying; it is an ethical act face to face with the
Other (Levinas, 1998b).[6] In that very instant preceding perception and cognition, the Saying is an embrace of the Other (Critchley, 1992; Peperzak,
1993). "The Saying is [. . .] the very enactment of the ethical movement
from the Same to the Other" (Critchley, 1992, p. 7).

The Saying is an exposure of the subject to the Other disruptive of
statements of cause and effect, linear narrative, and time. Contrary to the
discourse of Western ontology, the Saying cannot be characterized by the
patterns and rhythms of narrative order, hierarchy, or cause and effect. The

---

[4]Levinas's project is the exploration of the ethical conditions of possibility; it is a nonfoundational ethics that radically challenges the sovereignty of Western ontology emerging in the
cogito. For Levinas, what is radically otherwise is an asymmetrical relation that places responsibility for the other before the ego, before the sovereign individual, before the Being of
Western ontology. The epiphany of the face thus emerges through a prophetic discourse that
is otherwise than the ontology of Western philosophy, ". . . the relation to the face is straight
away ethical. The face is what one can not kill, or at least it is that whose meaning consists
in saying: 'thou shalt not kill'" (Levinas, 1985, p. 87). References in this context to "the ontology of 'Being'" refer to Levinas's project, following World War II and the Jewish Holocaust, to
deconstruct the work of his mentor, Martin Heidegger.
[5]First Landing of Christopher Columbus. Frederick Kemmelmyer. Oil on canvas, 1800-1805.
The National Gallery of Art. Washington, DC.
[6]References to the Saying refer to Levinas's linguistic turn in his later work, especially
Otherwise than Being or Beyond Essence originally published in 1974 (see Levinas, 1998b).

discourse of the Saying is intermittent and nonlinear. The Saying is not in time with beginning—middle—end because the time of the Saying is an immemorial time of diachrony. Relating diachrony to the ethical responsibility for the other, Levinas (1998a) wrote: "It is [. . .] a past that cannot be reduced to the present, that seems to signify in the ethical antecedent of responsibility-for-another-person, without reference to my identity . . ." (p. 150).

I cannot know or understand the instant of the face to face in Kemmelmyer's painting in terms of the historical present any more than I can understand the significance of Columbus as the Arawak did. Yet this face to face, this Saying, this actual historical instant is constitutive of my responsibility for the Other. In this instant, diverse futures are possible— were possible. Although 514 years later, what remains are only diverse histories and conflicting truths.

Incessantly interrupting Western discourse, the ethical Saying evades claims to comprehension and disables the pursuit of totalizing truths. The diachrony of the Saying hinders and suspends Western discourse. More important, Critchley (1992) wrote, "The Saying is a performative disruption . . . instantly refuted by the language in which it appears . . . " (p. 164). The ethical Saying vanishes in Western discourse only to emerge and emerge again to hinder and disrupt this same discourse, only to be instantly refuted. . . . In this way, the ethical Saying of Kemmelmyer's painting leaves its trace on a canvas of Western discourse at that very instant when Columbus stands face to face with the Arawak (Critchley, 1992).

THE DIACHRONY OF HYPERTEXT
AND THE ETHICAL SAYING

Borges' (1964) "The Garden of Forking Paths" is often referred to in discussions of the narrative conventions of time and linearity in hypertext (Bolter, 1991; Moulthrop, 1994; Moulthrop and Kaplin, 1994; Snyder, 1996). Although this celebrated short story describes German espionage and murder in Britain during World War I, it offers a narrative account of how a professor of English, Dr. Yu Tsun, came to understand the work of his great grandfather, Ts'ui Pên. As Borges explained, it was widely known that Ts'ui Pên retired as governor of Yunnan Province to write a great fictional account and to design the ultimate labyrinth. What was misunderstood until Yu Tsun discussed the matter with the British Sinologist, Stephen Albert, was that the fictional account is the ultimate labyrinth, its title, "The Garden of Forking Paths." The subject of this celebrated narrative/labyrinth is time, as the fictional character, Albert, explained:

> In all fictional works, each time a man is confronted with several alter-
> natives, he chooses one and eliminates the others; in the fiction of Ts'ui
> Pên, he chooses—simultaneously—all of them. He creates, in this way,
> diverse futures, diverse times which themselves also proliferate and
> fork. (p. 26)

The forking and intersecting paths of this labyrinth suggest the structural potential realized in hypertext. Indeed Borges' (1964) short story
becomes the object of Moulthrop's (1987) hypertext fiction, *Forking Paths*.
As the character Albert presages, Moulthrop (1987) retold and told anew, in
multiple variations, Borges' narrative of World War I espionage and murder. In the case of narrative fiction, as it is with historiography, linear time
functions as a trope; it is a metonym of lived experience. To disrupt this linear time would be to undermine the structure of the text, the sovereignty
of its subject, and perhaps the discipline as well. This capacity to disrupt
time is precisely what the medium of hypertext offers to its readers and
authors.

In the course I teach on hypertext design and curriculum theory, we
discuss Borges' (1964) work. There my pedagogy is informed, in part, by
the potential of hypertext, as a digital medium, to disrupt linearity and traditional hierarchy through linking practices and the juxtaposition of dissim-
ilar texts. However, even as the medium of hypertext is used to disrupt the
synchronous time of conventional linear narrative, hypertext does not form
a performative enactment of the ethical Saying. There is no medium to represent the face to face. It is beyond Western discourse. Even as the language of diachrony forms a metaphor of ethical responsibility, the face to
face defies the synchrony of Western thought.

At the same time, however tentative and conditional, I suggest an occasion for a homology between what I refer to as the diachrony of hypertext
and the diachrony of the face to face. Imploding the boundaries that would
distinguish hypertext technology, the conditions of its design, and the
experiences of its reader, a trace (or phantom or mirage) of the Saying can
remain in the diachrony of hypertext. This trace serves merely as an
ephemeral reminder of the ethical responsibiltiy of the self for the other.

The diachrony of hypertext is easily confused with a kind of technological determinism when considered within a critical discourse on hypertext
(Bolter, 1991; Joyce, 1995; Landow, 1997). Within this discourse, it is
argued that the multilinearity of the texts produced through the application
of hyperlinks challenges the sovereignty of the author and the tyranny of
textual hierarchies. In the field of education, it is claimed that hypertext is
a student-centered technology revealing the potential of constructivist pedagogy (Jonassen, 1998; Wilhelm, 1995). Further, there are reductionist
claims conflating the complexities of poststructural thought to the techni-

cal capacities of hypertext (Bolter, 1991; Landow, 1997; Turkle, 1995). With a multiplicity of links and paths to select when navigating through the screens of a hypertext, the reader is said to possess a newfound control of the writing space and the construction of meaning.

However, the majority of hypertext documents, such as those available on the World Wide Web, are structured hierarchies. Although a reader may determine her path through the web of a hypertext, this is too often reduced to determining a reading order and/or whether topical links are to be followed across the document. This is not unlike the use of linear indexing systems and tables of contents. In this way, "The First Americans" could be designed in a digital space as a hierarchical hypertext without presenting any challenge to its Eurocentric regime of representation.

Moulthrop's (1997) Web-based hypertext fiction, *Hegirascope*, offers a poignant corrective to this technological determinism as its design undermines assumptions about reader/text relations in hypertext. Although *Hegirascope* is designed with a multiplicity of links, the structure of its digital effects deliberately delivers control of the text and the reading experience back to the author. It becomes evident that reader control is not an essential quality of hypertext technology, but rather forms a continuum across the medium. There are no guarantees, cybernetic or otherwise. In Hegirascope, a new active window randomly pops up every 30 seconds severely undermining readerly control of the pace of the hypertext. Further, although there are usually multiple links on a given page, there is little readerly control over the reading path of this hypertext.

Readerly control then is not determined by the technology, but rather depends on an implosion of the boundaries distinguishing form from content and reader/text/writer interrelationships. This is suggested further in Odin's (1997) reading of Malloy's (1993) hypertext fiction, *Its Name Was Penelope*:

> As the reader goes through screen after screen, a few images keep recurring in different forms. . . . One such image is that of a boat named Penelope. . . . As the image is repeated, we see Ann launching other sailboats, even chasing after a small boat with her camera. . . . The concrete action of launching a boat and trying to capture the image of the boat coalesce in the realization that she cannot capture reality without transforming it. Any totalizing description remains forever elusive. (p. 608)

It is not the hyperlink that determines the significance of Malloy's (1993) fiction. Rather, it is relations between the hyperlink, what is written, and the subtle adjustments made to the text as it is encountered and read again and again by a reader forging her way through this specific hypertext.

This repeated encountering with a text that is adjusted, simultaneously, by design and through practices of the reader redefines the nonlinear in
hypertext. It is a nonlinearity that defies the synchrony or spatial representation of phenomena within a unified temporal order of cause and effect or
beginnings, middles, and ends (Critchley, 1992). The technical capacity of
hypertext to navigate a text with hyperlinks does not open a window onto
the world or onto a totality that can be known once and for all. Instead the
experience of hypertext begins to resemble an infinite and elusive world of
diachrony—an unrepeatable and immemorial time and an ephemeral and
unpredictable space (Critchley, 1992; Moulthrop, 1994; Odin, 1997).

A POSTCOLONIAL CRITIQUE
OF MULTICULTURALISM

> . . . the disruptive temporality of enunciation displaces the narrative of
> the Western nation . . .
>
> —Homi Bhabha (1995)

As Levinas reconstructed subjectivity as the responsibility for the Other, the
autonomy of the West is similarly reconstructed in postcolonial thought.
The subject of power—that familiar individual subject of Western ontology
and liberal humanism—is interpellated as rational, integral, and solely
responsible for her knowledge, beliefs and actions (Belsey, 1980; Hall,
1997; Henriques et al., 1984). However, as I introduced earlier, Levinas
(1985, 1996, 1998a, 1998b, 1998c) argued that prior to the sociocultural
production of this individual as a subject in discourse and prior to her conscious recognition of herself as an individual is her relation with the Other.
As an ethical face to face, this relation forms an unconditional responsibility for the Other (Levinas, 1998c). Levinas (1985) explained that this
responsibility does not form an arbitrary subject position; "Subjectivity is
not for itself; it is, once again, initially for another . . ." (p. 96). Subjectivity,
or the very capacity of being subjected, of being made a subject, is always
already for the Other. This relation of the subject of power to the Other
forms a central problematic in postcolonial thought and practices to desta-
bilize the sovereignty and autonomy of Western culture. The individual, as
the subject of power, forms a metonym that refers to the West. The essential attributes of this individual extend to broad reified categories of race,
gender, class, and the totality of the West (Bhabha, 1990).

The postcolonial critique of multiculturalism forms an instance of this
questioning of the totality of the West. Emerging later in chapter 1 of the
history textbook, "The First Americans" (*Beginnings to 1877*), and joined to

the regime of representation discussed earlier is an educational discourse on multiculturalism. This discourse functions to sustain the articulation of discrete and autonomous races, ethnicities, and cultures—what Trinh (1991) described as territorialized space. This understanding of cultural diversity is a central assumption of multiculturalism in which cultures are separated and distinguished from each other according to a contrived taxonomy of essential attributes and characteristics such as food, dress, housing, and medicine (McCarthy, 1998). Bhabha (1995) situated the discourse on multiculturalism within Eurocentric thought as he questioned practices of cultural diversity:

> Cultural diversity is an epistemological object—culture as object of empirical knowledge . . . a category of comparative ethics, aesthetics, or ethnology. . . . Cultural diversity is the recognition of pre-given cultural "contents" and customs, held in a time-frame of relativism. . . . Cultural diversity is also the representation of a radical rhetoric of the separation of totalized cultures . . . safe in the Utopianism of a mythic memory of a unique collective identity. (p. 206)

The multicultural layout and design of the chapter entitled "The First Americans" reproduces the dominant Western narrative of discovery while simultaneously constructing a mosaic of cultural diversity. The conceptual isolation of diverse cultures is reproduced through a textbook design that uses thick borders and shifting color schemes of text and background. Ironically, the multilinear design of this textbook, to a limited extent, mimics the hypertextual. In one instance, parallel to the discursive formation of the Western narrative is the story of an Acoma potter currently living in New Mexico.[7] As a fold in time across 1,000 years, a photograph of this potter, Ms. Lucy Lewis, shown working with clay, is surrounded by an archeological discourse on the practices of "Paleo-Indians." The caption beneath the photograph is used to anchor how she is to be understood (Barthes, 1977). It reads: "A renowned artist, Lewis follows a pottery tradition that is over 1,000 years old . . . the Acoma believe that creating pottery is a spiritual process. . . ." This textbook suggests a coherent and linear cultural history that has sustained the essential identity of the Acoma undisturbed by contact with other cultures. At the same time, the reader is implicitly invited to compare and contrast the Acoma with his assumed Eurocentric cultural identity.

---

[7]To interrupt this Western discourse, I quote from the Pueblo Acoma Sky City web site of the Acoma people, "The oral heritage of Acoma tells of the origin and migration of Acoma people in search of Hak'u. Acoma (pronounced either eh-Ko-Ma or Ah-Ko-Ma) is derived form the Keresan word Hak'u. It was prophesized from the beginning that a place existed for the acoma people to occupy" (Pueblo Acoma Sky City, 2004).

To disrupt this educational discourse on multiculturalism, McCarthy (1998) described the relational aspects of culture in a discussion of cultural hybridity. As a process, cultural hybridity occurs in a historically specific and lived contact zone where distinct cultures have come together (Pratt, 1992). This hybridity forms a third space (Bhabha, 1990, 1995) where the boundaries between one culture and a second culture are misrecognized. In this third space, cultures become deterritorialized (Trinh, 1991). Indeed as McCarthy (1998) wrote, " . . . the very definition of [a culture] depends on the existence and interaction with the other . . ." (p. 155). Further, to refuse any singular or identifiable origin of Western culture, McCarthy (1998) wrote, " . . . the other is always already present in notions of the West" (p. 158). As it concerns the mutual conditioning and coproduction characterizing cultural relations, hybridity refuses any linear historiography or fold in time that would search for origins to identify, once and for all, the pure essence that determines and distinguishes a culture from other cultures (Bhabha, 1995).

CONCLUSION

On first encountering the unfamiliar and disorienting medium of hypertext, a reader's attention is often distracted away from issues of content and drawn to issues of form or structure. Although distinctions between form and content in hypertext ultimately implode, if only for an instant, the separation affords a pedagogic opportunity for what Moulthrop (1994) described as "looking at a medium." In the courses I teach, I take advantage of this opportunity to focus on and explore with students the form and construction of hypertext. At the same time, it is this implosion that is of greater concern in discussions of hypertext as it is in postcolonial thought and the ethical.

Extending the homology of diachrony, from hypertext and the ethical to postcolonial thought, in this third space Western assumptions of linear time and cultural diversity are disrupted. This third space is a contradictory space—an ambivalent space that refuses hierarchical claims to cultural origins and purities and subverts Western narratives of history and multiculturalism (Bhabha, 1995). Emerging from this third space, there is no reified culture or nation fixed in its unique and linear development to be known once and for all.

In its rendering of the first encounter of Columbus and the Arawak peoples, Kemmelmyer's painting emerges in this third space. It is a Saying, if only for an instant, as the reader bears witness to the face of the Other. However, in the final instant, the Saying is not located in the synchronous time of Western discourse (Bhabha, 1995; Peperzak, 1993). Instead the very possibility of an ethical language of the Saying is exactly what cannot be reduced to Western discourse. This elusive relation of the subject to the Other that defines ethical responsibility for Levinas emerges only in an ephemeral moment because it is pursued and pursued again and again. In the third space of an immemorial past, the First Landing of Christopher Columbus forms a trace of an ethical responsibility for the Other.

As I presented in this chapter, there is a homology among this ethical responsibility, postcolonial thought, and the medium of hypertext. This homology suggests strategies for reconstructing history texts in webbed environments using hypertext, a medium marked by recursion and multiplicity. Emphasizing an ephemeral relation of the self to the Other, these strategies are relational, situated, nonlinear, and overflowing of the formal boundaries of Western narrative and historiography.

REFERENCES

Africans In America (2003). Retrieved October 22, 2003, from www.pbs.org/aia.

Barthes, R. (1977). *Image: Music: Text*. New York: The Noon Day Press.

Belsey, C. (1980.) *Critical practice*. New York: Methuen.

Bhabha, H. (1990). The third space. Interview with J. Rutherford. In J. Rutherford (Ed.), *Identity: Community, culture, difference* (pp.207–221). London: Lawrence & Wishart.

Bhabha, H. (1995). Cultural diversity and cultural differences. In B. Ashcroft, G. Griffiths, & H. Tiffin (Eds.), *The post-colonial studies reader* (pp. 206–214). New York: Routledge.

Bolter, J. D. (1991). *The writing space: The computer, hypertext, and the history of writing*. Hillside, NJ: Lawrence Erlbaum Associates.

Borges, J. (1964). *Labyrinths: Selected stories and other writings*. New York: New Directions.

Center for World Indigenous Studies Forum for Global Exchange, Fourth World Documentation Program. (2003). Retrieved October 22, 2003, from http://www.cwis.org/fwdp/290%20FWDP/index.html

Critchley, S. (1992). *The ethics of deconstruction: Derrida & Levinas*. Cambridge, MA: Blackwell.

Hall, S. (1997). *Representation: Cultural representations and signifying practices*. Thousand Oaks, CA: Sage.

Harding, S. (1998). *Is science multicultural: Postcolonialisms, feminisms, and epistemologies*. Bloomington: Indiana University Press.

Henriques, J., Hollway, W., Urwin, C., Venn, C., and Walkerdine, V. (1984). *Changing the subject: Psychology, social regulation and subjectivity*. New York: Methuen.

Jonassen, D. (1998). *Computers in the classroom: Mindtools for critical thinking*. Columbus, OH: Merrill.

Joyce, M. (1995). *Of two minds: Hypertext pedagogy and poetics*. Ann Arbor: University of Michigan Press.

Landow, G. (1997). *Hypertext 2.0.* Baltimore, MD: Johns Hopkins University Press.

Levinas, E. (1998a). *Entre nous: On thinking-of-the-other* (M. B. Smith & B. Harshav, Trans.). New York: Columbia University Press.

Levinas, E (1998b). *Otherwise than being or beyond essence* (A. Lingis, Trans.). Pittsburgh: Duquesne University Press.

Levinas, E. (1998c). *Totality and infinity* (A. Lingis, Trans.). Pittsburgh: Duquesne University Press.

Levinas, E. (1996). *Basic philosophical writings* (A. Peperzak, S. Critchle, & R. Bernasconi, Eds.). Bloomington: Indiana University Press.

Levinas, E. (1985). *Ethics and infinity, conversations with Philippe Nemo* (R. Cohen, Trans.). Pittsburgh: Duquesne University Press.

Malloy, J. (1993). *It's name was Penelope.* Cambridge, MA: Eastgate Systems.

Malmsheimer, L. (1985). Imitation White man: Images of transformation at the Carlisle Indian School. *Studies in Visual Communication, 11*(4). 54–75.

McCarthy, C. (1998). *The uses of culture: Education and the limits of ethnic affiliation.* New York: Routledge.

Moulthrop, S. (1997). *Hegirascope: A hypertext fiction.* Retrived October 21, 2003, from http://www.cddc.vt.edu/journals/newriver/moulthrop/HGS2/Hegirascope. html.

Moulthrop, S. (1994). Rhizome and resistance: Hypertext and the dreams of a new culture. In G. P. Landow (Ed.), *Hyper/text/theory* (pp. 299–322). Baltimore: Johns Hopkins University Press..

Moulthrop, S. (1987). *Forking paths.* Unpublished hypertext fiction.

Moulthrop, S., & Kaplan, N. (1994). They became what they beheld: The futility of resistance in the space of electronic writing. In C. L. Selfe & S. Hilligoss (Eds.), *Literacy and computers: The complications of teaching and learning with technology* (pp. 220–237). New York: The Modern Language Association.

Odin, J. (1997). The edge of difference: Negotiations between the hypertextual and the postcolonial. *Modern Fiction Studies, 43*(3), 598–630.

Peperzak, A. (1993). *To the Other: An introduction to the philosophy of Emmanuel Levinas.* West Lafayette, IN: Purdue University Press.

Pueblo Acoma Sky City. (2004). Retrieved June 17, 2004, from www.puebloofacoma.org/index2.htm.

Pratt, M. (1992). *Imperial eyes: Travel writing and transculturation.* New York: Routledge.

Rethinking schools online. (2003). Retrieved October 22, 2003 from http://www. rethinkingschools.org/.

Rosaldo, R. (1993). *Culture & truth: The remaking of social analysis.* Boston: Beacon.

Snyder, I. (1996). *Hypertext: The electronic labyrinth.* New York: New York University Press.

The circle: News and art from a Native American perspective. (2003). Retrieved October 22, 2003, from http://www.thecirclenews.org/.

Trinh, M. (1991). *When the moon waxes red.* New York: Routledge.

Turkle, S. (1995). *Life on the screen: Identity in the age of the Internet.* New York: Simon & Schuster.

Wilhelm, J. (1995). Creating the missing links: Student-designed learning on hypermedia. *English Journal, 84*(6), 34–40.

6

NEW MEDIA, REPRESENTATION, AND EDUCATION

Robert Muffoletto

Editor's note: New digital media and the Internet are better understood in a historical context where all media have brought about various sociocultural changes. This chapter addresses the idea that representation and remediation of the other, by and through various representational technologies and media forms, construct the identity of the self through the construction of the other. The use of the new media offers the opportunity for education to become multicultural.

How we come to know the world, ourselves, and others in it is the result of various forms of mediation, representation, remediation, and cultural discourses. The digital media technologies (system of representation) of the 21st century have their roots in the development and democratization of the photographic image and its ability to mediate the self and others that appear to be seamless, transparent, and accurate. The signifier, the representation in image and sound, presented is believed to be a truthful and accurate rendering and portrayal of the real.

From the articulate daguerreotype to the cell phone Web cam, from the O'Sullivan images of Gettysburg to the reporter with the troops in Iraq, the image has given us what we have wanted—a look at the other, a report from the field, a definition of oneself.

In this chapter, I argue that the emerging digital technologies and communication systems are a continuation of the efforts to define and represent the other and us in light of ideological steerage and solidification. Education as a multicultural arena, struggling to define itself within a conserving ideological framework, needs to address the institutional definitions of the individual and community in light of knowledge, world, and truth making. To accomplish this, I situate multicultural education (education that is multicultural) within a vision of the new media and a global education that is democratic, community centered, and nonoppressive.

Before discussing the new digital media and the Internet, we need to situate the new media within a historical framework of image making and representation. Not to do this, even in a minimal manner, would remove the nature of media from any social historical construct. Images of self and others did not just happen—the camera-produced image emerged at a time of colonialism, the beginnings of tourism, a growing and expanding middle class, and a growing curiosity of self and the world. The year 1839 historically marked when Daguerre announced his image-making invention— the Daguerreotype. As with contemporary representational photography, the Daguerreotype was referred to, in its day, as a mirror of reality. It was so detailed that every hair and every wrinkle of the sitter could be counted. It was faster and more accurate than any painter could create. The photographic image became more than a reflection of reality; it became truth.

The Daguerreotype was affordable to many who could not afford the cost of a likeness produced by a sitting painter (Newhall, 1964). This mirror of nature emerged at a time when empiricism and positivism were becoming deeply embedded in the consciousness of the Western modern world. The camera was seen as a machine—a product of science and the innovative nature of man. The Daguerreotype, a new media of the mid-19th century, changed the menu concerning representation and remediation of reality. The Daguerreotype and the analog systems that followed in the late 18th and 20th centuries, provided a foundation for the emerging new digital multimedia systems that "define us and them" in an increasing global network.

Photography and its role as a new media is best understood within a sociocultural context. Like other new media of the 19th and 20th centuries the camera-made image, reflecting the intelligence of the camera operator, had major effects on the consciousness of the general public. As a fixed form of representation, the camera-made illusion impacted information storage and retrieval, notions of evidence and history, business, and education. The still image flowed into other image-making formats. The stereograph, movies (film), TV, the holographic image, and the computer-generated, three-dimensional, digital virtual reality all trace their history back to

1839, the mirror image, and the nature of representation and truth. As a form of representation, the photograph with the printing press is the foundation for the control and mass dissemination of images of the other. The other as seen and understood, constructed for consumption, and for the gaze of dominance is a major concern for an educational system that strives to be multicultural, democratic, and inclusive.

Other new media of the day changed and expanded forms of communication and information storage and exchange. How people knew about, understood, and constructed the other as well as the self was impacted and formed by the emergence of the new media of the day. In thinking of new media, we need to realize that at some historical moment, all old media were new (Gitelman & Geoffrey, 2003). The telegraph, telephone, film, radio, phonographs, audio recording, and storage systems (tape recorders), TV, videocamcorders, computers, and fax machines were at one time objects of the new media. They all eventually became media or old media as newer forms emerged out of the current forms.

Each development in media not only affected our sensory system, but also as McLuhan (1964) stated decades ago, became extensions of ourselves, extending our consciousness backward and forward in time and space. The telegraph and radio became our voice, the camera our memory, and the TV our eyes and a window to a world. The computer, the new media of the latter part of the 20th century, through digitalization and convergence of analog media, changed what Negroponte (1995) referred to as atoms into bits, from physical objects to space. The convergence of analog media into one format, the digital, changed, as photography did, the menu of representation and remediation.

Today's new digital media is different from what may be called old media or analog media. Analog media presents or delivers gradate information all at once. Photographs, like other analog media, provided access to their coded information (representations of image or sound) all at one time. Audiotapes, TV, film (movies), and radio are examples of analog media that emerged out of the 18th century and the need to see and hear a world removed from its actual context. Concerns over the veracity, mediation, and remediation of phenomena accompanied each new media as it appeared on the technological and social horizon.

Different from analog, digital media (images and sounds) are codified in a binary structure. Binary code is formatted in a series of 1s and 0s or in a "on or off" system. Similar to the use of *dots* and *dashes* (Morse code) encoded and decoded by telegraph operators, digital media is encoded by a programmer to be decoded by a computer processor and displayed on a user interface—a monitor of sorts. In this binary format, digital media is coded all the same; there is no difference in how audiovisual information is encoded and decoded to a computer screen. In this manner, images, texts, and sounds can be combined, moved, and copied in one format, allowing for easy manipulation, dissemination, and consumption (Flew, 2002).

It is the computer—the processor of the binary code—that represents through an interface device called a screen (or, in the case of sound, via a speaker interface). The screen interface is the surface that allows the user to interact with the program. We are surrounded by representations displayed by screen interfaces: TV screens, movie screens, hand-held (PDA) computers, ATM screens, and computer screens. It is the screen that acts as an interface, a surface of presentation and representation, between the processed code and the viewer. Media's purpose, new or old, is to produce and reproduce representations as the reconstruction of a world managed (and distributed) through a non-neutral media format, one that is loaded with a rich history of manipulation and dissemination of information and worldviews.

The power of the new digital media is the compression and convergence of analog media into one format. Once in a common format or code, images, sounds, films, and text can be moved around, copied and pasted, combined together, and edited to construct what is termed *multimedia*. (To refer to images, sounds, and text is misleading. What is actually being referred to is the code behind the interface. It is the code that is manipulated and disseminated through the interface of the screen surface. We need to remember that it is the code that produces what we experience. From this perspective, the image does not exist as an object in real space and time, but as a surface between the viewer and the code.) The computer has become a multimedia interface that presents the user with various mediated forms of information. Digital media, new media, builds on a convergence of media types and networking through the computer. Before the emergence of the digital format, analog multimedia presentations would include slide projectors and slides, film and film projectors, reel-to-reel audiotape players, and a controlling device to manage all of the delivery devices. Digital media converged all of these formats and devices into one—the computer that processes the code and generates the image to be consumed (visual and sound).

Combine multimediated information with a broadband computer network and there is the potential for a high-speed delivery system that can provide the same mediated message to every computer and user on the Internet or the World Wide Web (WWW). There is also the potential for interaction between users that before the WWW was slow, clumsy, and usually limited to one mediated format (letters as text, audiotape, and still and moving images—film and photographs). In terms of educational uses of the global networked digital media, there is the potential for a standardized, centrally controlled curriculum delivered to every user/learner connected to the Internet. From another perspective, there is the opportunity for an interactive environment promoting communication that supports one to many and many to one, bringing a dynamic potential for learning and creating a democratic and robust environment, allowing for the development of a multicultural curriculum.

The point in saying all of this about old and new media, atoms and bits, is to begin to create in a context for understanding the impact of new and old media on education, and specifically an education's knowledge system—an educational system that many are struggling to make multicultural in both content and context. Public education as a social institution, charged with educating all youth to become productive citizens (which usually means developing skills for success in the world of labor and not questioning, but respecting authority), reflected and legitimized only certain ways of knowing and being in the world (Apple, 1979; Callahan, 1962; Kliebard, 1987; Spring, 1986). Media, in all of its formats, reflected the purpose of education as a tool of the educational system.

New media, as introduced throughout the 20th century, promised (actually those who would benefit from it use and consumption made the promises) to solve various educational challenges as defined by the system. From Edison's proclamation that films would replace textbooks, to the use of educational TV to address weak teachers and inequalities in the efficient dissemination of curricular content (Cuban, 1986; Muffoletto, 2001), new media was positioned as a scientific and engineered solution to a series of problems facing public education. The field of educational technology (also known as instructional technology) emerged from the confines defined as *audiovisual aids*, to educational technology, defined by concepts in science and engineering.

Before the 1940s, media was used as an aid to teachers and students in the classroom. After World War II, audiovisual aids shifted to a systematic or technology of instruction. There is a major shift at this time from the concept of an aid controlled by the teacher to a delivery system controlled by the system. It was the merging of a psychology of learning with system concepts borrowed from engineering to address the perceived needs of society for an efficient and effective educational system. The new educational analog media of the 1960s—TV, audio recorders, portable video recorders, and others—merged with packaged instructional materials to form a curricular delivery system that repositioned teachers and redefined the skills required of teaching. The 1960s was a time of struggles for civil rights, Viet Nam, walks on the moon, the Beatles and Elvis, White flight to the suburbs, the cold war, and Skinner's teaching machine. The 1960s led into the 1970s, 1980s, and 1990s, with a movement back to the basics, the development of affordable desktop computers and software, national panels inquiring in to the conditions of public education, state-level teacher tests, and the early stages of integrated learning systems as a technology of control over the minds of students and the behaviors of teachers. The second half of the 20th century also marked the struggles by marginalized communities to break from a tightly woven curriculum based upon a Western European consciousness to a curriculum recognizing the changing nature of truth as formed by postmodern thought and the diversity found in the world—multiculturalism.

As public education moves through the early years of the 21st century, it is faced with a questionable teaching force and a growing classroom teacher shortage as a result of a perceived public value of teachers, and the nature of the profession to attract and hold teachers in the classroom. Couple this condition with a growing parent population looking to alternative schooling because of either a loss of faith in public education to meet the needs of their children or conservative religious rejection of the secular school curriculum. Since the 1950s, symbolized by Skinner's teaching machine and systematic design for the delivery of the curriculum (Trow, 1963), and the programmed instructional kits of the 1960s, the institution of schooling has been exploring mediated systems to bring education under control as an effective social institution and to standardize distribution and content of the curriculum.

The new digital media of the 21st century offers the system or technology through which this can be accomplished. It is not difficult to convince the general population who still understand schooling as a vehicle to a better life for their children (or to maintain the current socioeconomic status of the family) and to draw on the potential new digital multimedia (which is associated with science, progress, and opportunity) to deliver content and evaluate learners. The efforts to establish a technology of control over the constants and variables of the classroom took form in the "Leave No Child Behind Act" (NCLB). The act sets the stage for a national standardized curriculum and delivery through integrated learning systems. It is within this set of arrangements that those who struggle to make education multicultural in form and content must do battle.

I use the term *battle* to signify the struggles of those who have been marginalized or excluded from the school curriculum in favor of a more conservative, mainstream curriculum presenting primarily a Western view of the world by the centering of a Western European culture and its values. Cultural wars over the lived experience, culture, and values of students and teachers are not a debate over just primary language (English as the official language, marginalizing all others) and the celebration of holidays; it is about White, Western European, and Christian privilege (Apple, 2001; Shor, 1992; Sleeter, 1996), the valuing of different historical stories, and asking critical and reflective questions concerning the social, political, and economic conditions that have an effect on the lives of people inside and out of the United States.

As I suggested earlier, the conditions found at the end of the 20th century were favorable for a rethinking of education and the delivery of its curriculum in the United States. Through the development of new digital media integrated learning systems, the loss of faith of classroom teachers and the ability of public schooling to teach children in an effective manner and a safe environment, the inability of the profession to attract and retain qualified and experienced teachers in the classroom, and the growth of nationalism and fear as a result of the events on September 11, 2001, technologies of control seem reasonable and necessary. Programs that report to potentially help the middle and working class and working poor, by providing their children with richer educational opportunities while striving to make the educational system work for them, receive the full support of many segments of the population. Who can argue with the overt intent of the NCLB and a integrated learning system that draws on the new digital interactive media and the Internet to create what is proclaimed as effective, efficient, and accountable learning environments for children and communities. Within this context, the standardized test plays a critical role in defining what learning is and how we know that the student has learned the required content of the curriculum.

Within this context of a technology of control—attempts to hear many voices, to offer diverse perspectives on the world from the world, and to make education multicultural—is a struggle as the educational system is beckoned into a conservative Christian right framework (Apple, 1996, 2001; Shor, 1992). Taking the attributes of the new media—digitalization, convergence, and networking—and using them to construct and maintain a diverse learning environment that values inquiry, analysis, and participation into "rich and thick" understandings of the world creates another view of learning and schooling. Employing the use of the new media, its interactivity and global perspective, to investigate and understand how a controlled societal point of view is disseminated and controlled by those behind the messages delivered through mass media, education, churches, and families impact the social, economic, and political consciousness of the consuming population. It is within this context that education becomes multicultural, borderless, and decentered.

Within a conserving technology of control (conserving the status quo) that strives to maintain gender, economic, and racial relations that benefit those that have, we normally hear a single voice, receive a packaged construct of the world, and read the definition of the individual within it. The subjectivity of the individual within a conserving ideology is nonhistorical and exists outside the dialectical. The world and ourselves in it are given to us as a curriculum with one truth, one history, and one world as seen through the lens of those who benefit from the way the world is.

To decenter education from its historical roots, to make it multicultural, is not an easy task. In the past, educational media, used by school administration, was envisioned to bring order and structure to the school day and the delivery of the state-approved legitimate curriculum. The use of educational TV to deliver the curriculum by master teachers and a teacher's guide that accompanied the approved textbook steered the delivery of the curriculum by the classroom teacher. As the system expanded into programmed materials and kits, the teacher did not require fundamental knowledge of the content—it was all in the teacher's guidebook. SRA kits, which repositioned the teacher as a manager of the classroom, worked to deskill the classroom teacher by repositioning the instructional decisions to the designers of the kit. In the nearer past (late 1970s, 1980s, and into the 1990s), we find the use of the early computer programs designed to deliver (CBI), assist (CAI), and manage (CMI) the distribution of the curriculum. As we enter into the 21st century, the development of interactive digital technologies, the Internet, and the NCLB raised the bar on innovation, creativity, and diversity of thought and knowledge. The pressure is on teachers to perform, for schools to be successful, and for children to learn what is to be tested. The challenge is to understand what it means for schools to work, for children to learn, and who and what benefits from those definitions.

In a period of growing conservatism and extreme nationalism, the flexibility of teachers to mold the curriculum and engage her students in regional, national, and global conversations, through the new media and the Internet while addressing global issues with others in the world, is becoming more difficult except for the more affluent schools. As the logic of the system further defines what it means to be educated, to know, and to act, it is the system (the ideological behind the system) driving educational practice. If that practice is camouflaged in the rhetoric of progress, standards, accountability, governmental responsibility, choice, and national interest, the classroom teacher, the local school administrator, and school board member will find it difficult to unpack the discourse in light of public demands for schools that work for their children.

Educators pursuing an education that is multicultural will have a difficult time justifying expenditures of time and resources to build a conversation on a national or global scale. At a time when middle-class parents are concerned that the same opportunities that were available for them will not be available for their children, and the working class and working poor are trying to keep the door open for their children's future, questioning a system that promotes leaving no child behind is a monumental task. Add to this the concerns over student Internet access (in an attempt to protect children) and you have a system that restrains the creative and collaborative use of the new media network to build diversification and a global consciousness.

Education that is multicultural questions the status quo of education in the United States. To address issues and questions related to diversity, access to knowledge and information (because both terms are so broad in meaning, I do not attempt to define them, but to code them with meaning within the context of my text), truth, and community building is a political reaction to the walled-in, test-driven classrooms found in many public school classrooms. Teachers have expressed concerns to me about the growing stress levels in their jobs. In North Carolina, teachers and administrators may be removed from schools by the state if their school's end-of-year test scores do not show improvement over a number of years. As a reward for teaching to the test, teachers' pay increases are based on improved test scores. Public opinion of the local school is greatly influenced by school report cards. Sitting with parents and students at parent conferencing times will take on a different level of discussion based on the schools test scores and the perceived value of their children's schooling experience.

In some communities where factories and business have either closed down or moved away to locations where labor costs less, it becomes easy to blame the other for your problems and not corporate and federal policies. The other, usually in this case, is the Black, Hispanic, or some other newly arrived group to a community. For teachers to propose curriculum that strives to value and understand cultures and views from outside the mainstream of thought in the United States may meet with resistance by the locals. For education to be multicultural, it must promote democratic principles and contextualize the curriculum in stories of equality and struggles. Multicultural education only needs to be reactionary and proactive until it becomes normalized. When the need to confront inequalities and social injustices within a democratic model guided by law is eliminated, education will be multicultural. When education in the United States understands itself within a context of no borders and global perspectives, it will be multicultural. To function in this manner, education must either re-create the test to reflect diverse ways of being in the world or create methods of curricular intervention and the valuing of an education that is multicultural.

One aspect of the new digital media beyond the convergence of various media forms and the networking capabilities of the Internet is its potential to eliminate borders and the tendency to centralize control over the storage and dissemination of information (Flew, 2002).

The new media, networked on a global scale, has great potential in building communities of practice and learning communities where diverse forms of knowledge are shared and valued. Communities of practice and learning communities share the quest for diversity and collectivity. Communities of practice bring individuals together to build on each other's knowledge and experiences—a community representing various elements and drawn together for a common purpose and vision.

In the past, learning communities were defined by geography and ease of communication. The telegraph of the 19th century offered the possibility to go beyond business transactions and individual exchanges, to identifying and building a network of individuals who were interested in sharing and learning from a collective (Gitelman & Geoffrey, 2003). Scientific and engineering academies, which once only knew of colleagues' work through published books and journals, gained access to ideas and information as the communication technologies became faster and broader. What at one time may have taken months or years for a book or scientific journal to travel from one side of Europe to another changed with advancing transportation and delivery networks. Information, in the 19th and early 20th century would be disseminated and exchanged at the speed of a cross-Atlantic steamer, the cross-continental railroad, on the back of a pony (pony express), or at the finger tips of a telegraph operator. Later the telephone and airplane, the radio signal and TV, and the satellite and digital media impacted not only the speed of information dissemination but also the nature of that information. What could be moved over telegraph lines is different than what can be disseminated through the Internet.

The nature and use of information in the social world are determined not only by its context, but by its form of dissemination and its logical structures of the system employed (Brown & Duguid, 2002; Flew, 2002). The Internet, a network of decentralized computers, and the new media create the environment for communities of practice to form and share information in text, still and moving images, and sound, at the speed of light dislocating the traditional sense of geography and time. The networked new media not only provided outsiders a view in, but a vehicle for insiders to get information out.

Digital media and the Internet have the ability, if so used, to create borderless learning communities. Within an educational program, which is multicultural, the opportunities offered by the design and use of networked learning communities to situate learners within an environment that values diversity and the intellectual tradition of inquiry and critique decenters the voice of authority to "voices of understandings." Learning communities designed to use the shared knowledge of the global network move out of a framework valuing localism and regionalism to one that entertains broader perspectives on the question at hand.

Learning communities, if so designed, engage individuals from diverse racial, ethnic, and linguistic traditions in the pursuit of knowing. In doing so, the learning of skills and knowledge, the acquiring of information, moves away from a central education system to a borderless and open investigation. The Internet is built on the notion of interaction and exchange of information, ideas, and perspectives. Learning communities, that value different cultural and historical stories support a horizontal exchange, with interaction occurring between students, students–teachers, and students–teacher–others (others being from outside the traditional structure of the school). In this model, the learning framework and the students' expectations and understandings value and invite various viewpoints.

CHANGING THE MENU

The use of media, new or old, as an attachment to current practice will not in the end affect anything. Since the 1990s, educational and business leaders have called for the integration of computer technology into the daily practice of teachers and learners. Little mention is made of the impact of computer technology on the day-to-day lives of teachers and students and the culture of the classroom. Little attention is given to the menu of classroom activities.

In the 1960s in the city of Greensboro, North Carolina (USA), at the early beginnings of the civil rights movement in the United States, Black Americans staged sit-ins at diners and cafes in an attempt to gain access to the same lunch counter as their fellow White citizens. The eventual integration of the lunch counter not only spirited the civil rights movement, but also, in a symbolic manner, changed the diner's menu. The same must be realized for education. Computer related-technologies cannot be brought into the classroom without changing, in a sense, the menu. If nothing changes and teachers and students experience more of the same, school leaders can boast of the digital technologies in their schools as a sign of progress and being progressive, but in a day-to-day sense the classroom menu remains the same. If schools do not function differently as an effect of the appearance of new media, if different messages are not given as to what it means to learn and teach, the menu may be more colorful, but the selection is still the same, and the bill is higher.

DIGITAL MEDIA
AND MULTICULTURAL EDUCATION

If schools do embrace a new menu, a new operational system, and a curriculum (overt and covert) that is reflective in image as well as practice of multiculturalism, what could networked digital media offer to that vision? Earlier I briefly discussed some ideas concerning communities of practice and learning communities, and how they may impact a classroom or school—using the Internet to develop learning communities that represent a broader population, not only of racial, ethnic, religious, economic, and gender, but the understanding about oneself and others in relationship to the environment of an online learning community. To build a learning community and understand its implications and culture takes time and patience. Foremost, a learning community that reproduces the current status, keeping a Euro-centered curriculum and teacher-centered learning environment built on "right" answers to questions already answered, moves schooling back to where it was. To use the Internet to build a diverse community that beckons students to a worldview that privileges a White, male-centered, upper middle-class world does not support an education that is multicultural. For global learning communities to work, to broaden the views and understandings of everyone in the community, diverse voices need to be heard and valued. The idea of *horizontal exchanges* is pivotal in that the power relationships are flattened, allowing every voice credence, offering at some level resistance to Western White male domination of ideas and values. The covert function of a diverse community may be to reveal the taken-for-granted or commonsense knowledge of Western European thought presented as the *truth* in the schooling experience.

Other aspects of the new media (networked) on education that questions and resists the current paradigm offered by the LNCB includes: releasing students from the function of consumers of information to the responsibility of creating knowledge; the development of partnerships between the learning community and other institutions and individuals; and promoting increased representation of ideas, histories, values, and visions for the future. Networked communities do not need to be global in structure; schools can create communities on local, regional, national, and global levels. The point is that the learning communities need to be multicultural in concept and practice. If they are not, the conversation will be one way, walled in by oppressive borders, marginalizing intellectual pursuit and inquiry, and socializing others in ways that benefit the dominant ideological order of being. To be a learning community, the community must allow full citizenship, access to their own voice and representation, and open interaction and exchanges among all members. The management and regulation of content must evolve out of the community and not be walled in by conservative beliefs, worldviews, and convenience (Sleeter, 1996). In doing so, the community as a socializing agent will construct individuals who may offer as a collective resistance to nondemocratic and nonequalitarian practices.

The new digital media (networked or not) and its convergence of various media forms into one interchangeable format allow the user to construct messages or representations in more powerful and challenging ways. Once they are connected to the Internet, the accessibility of their voice is available to anyone on the "grid" who wants to listen. We have historically thought of writers as typically working with words—text on paper or text on screen. The new media allows the integration of other forms of representation, including text, sound or audio, and still and moving images. Each format is a form of writing, meaning making, and representation. It provides to the author of the text new ways to conceptualize, express, and disseminate his or her voice. It provides the reader of the text the opportunity to engage the intelligence of the author. The new media, if networked and designed for providing avenues of interaction, provides an environment for communication and critical and reflective exchanges between authors and readers. The multimediated text becomes the interface between the consciousness and intellect of the writer and reader. (I draw the terms author, text and reader from postmodernist and semiotic theories related to the author and reader.) Similar to the integration of the lunch counter or the food store, the menu is changed, the shelves are stocked with different foods and if you look closely, the food store is starting to be organized, reflecting a new consciousness.

As I suggested earlier, the movement of education to adopt a new menu—a menu that serves knowledge, skills, and information that reflects the multidimensional, diverse cultural and historical cultural frameworks of the people of the world and the political and economic conditions they live in, and asks why conditions are the way they are—is an act of resistance to the conservative, Western European intellectual tradition. Curriculum, as it is now practiced, is camouflaged under a net of science, neutrality, and extreme individualism (Apple, 1982) that sets a narrow horizon line defining who we are and, just as important, who they are.

CONCLUSION

The new media by itself will not change schools or make education multicultural. To effect change, communities that value diversity and social justice need to drive the use of the interactive digital media. Just as the institution of schooling is framed by the logic of the institution (Apple, 1996; Berger & Luckmann, 1966; Flew, 2002), organizing learners perceptions of themselves and their futures to fit the ideological constructs of its constructed reality, so does the mass media of TV, radio, and print. For example, my grandmother (bless her heart) watched televised wrestling every Saturday back in the 1950s, and she believed, or at least she told me she believed, that it was real. In similar fashion, we are currently swimming through a rash of "reality TV" programs that have very little to do with reality outside the screen, except for the reality of the produced program. I am not suggesting that schooling is like reality TV, although the comparison would be interesting to explore. But like realty TV, the curriculum is constructed to steer the learner to notions of truth and importance. For what becomes important is embedded in word and image in the curriculum and on the test. It is the test that legitimizes and steers the curriculum and the valued knowledge and skills within. Similar to reality TV, we give ourselves over to the text and the image.

Digital media, especially digital media networked over the Internet, provides a format for education to move in a global perspective by providing a networked educational system that insists on social equality, situates Western thought on an equal basis with other conceptual and economic frameworks, and attempts to counter oppressive racist, sexist, religious, and economic practices. It is a different perspective from one that supports a corporate globalization and a colonizing hegemony of Western ideological realities. Because of the ease with which individuals and communities can employ the new media for global communication (e-mail, listservs chats, discussion boards) and the production and dissemination of powerful multimedia presentations (Web sites, PowerPoint, streaming video, CDs and DVD disks) through applications similar to "I-Movie" and "Movie Maker," in combination with information collected through digital still and moving cameras, digital audio recording devices, as well as word processors and text editors, messages that counter or challenge commonsense ideas and practices can be produced and disseminated to an international audience at very little expense. In the same vain, messages that present, similar to reality TV, postcards and cruise ship tours—stories that construct social conditions as nonoppressive, showing images of happy and healthy natives—can be produced and disseminated as well, hiding the conditions behind the camera.

Education that is multicultural and inquires into the nature of human life and social conditions will prepare students, as well as teachers, to unpack these messages through dialog and communication with others. To achieve this condition, we need to follow the example of the NCLB—that is, test for it.

At the start of this chapter, I used the invention of photography to refer to change caused by a new media. Photography not only freed art from its historical role of representation and depiction, but it also initiated changes in social behavior and concepts of the self. It was not until the invention of the Kodak camera by George Eastman that we find a population able to record itself in easy and eventually anticipated ways. The new digital media of the late 20th century, and now the early 21st century, has initiated cognitive and social behavioral change. New media has allowed our consciousness to go almost everywhere and be everywhere (McLuhan & Powers, 1989). The impact of this condition has not yet affected education in any meaningful manner; as a social institution, schooling is slow to change and adapt to new possibilities. What the new digital media does offer to education is the potential of being networked and in "touch" with the minds of others. To an educational system that is multicultural and focused on issues related to democracy and social justice, the new media provides a structure to hear the voices of others and to be heard.

REFERENCES

Apple, M. (1979). *Ideology and curriculum*. London: Routledge & Kegan Paul.

Apple, M. (1982). *Education and power*. Boston: ARK Press.

Apple, M. (1996). *Cultural politics & education*. New York: Teachers College Press.

Apple, M. (2001). *Educating the "right" way: Markets, standards, God, and inequality*. New York: Routledge Falmer.

Berger, P., & Luckmann, T. (1966). *The social construction of reality*. New York: Anchor Books.

Brown, J., & Duguid, P. (2002). *The social life of information*. Boston: Harvard Business School Press.

Callahan, R. (1962). *Education and the cult of efficiency*. Chicago: University of Chicago Press.

Cuban, L. (1986). *Teachers and machines: The classroom use of technology since 1920*. New York: Teachers College Press.

Flew, T. (2002). *New media: An introduction*. Oxford: Oxford University Press.

Gitelman, L., & Geoffrey, G. (2003). *New media, 1740–1915*. Cambridge, MA: MIT Press.

Kliebard, H. (1987). *The struggle for the American curriculum 1893–1958*. New York: Routledge.

McLuhan, M. (1964). *Understanding media: The extensions of man*. New York: McGraw-Hill.

McLuhan, M., & Powers, R. (1989). *The global village: Transformations in world life and media in the 21st century*. Oxford: Oxford University Press.

Muffoletto, R. (2001). The need for critical theory and reflective practices in educational technology. In R. Muffoletto (Ed.), *Education & technology: Critical and reflective practices* (pp. 285-299). Cresskill, NJ: Hampton Press.

Negroponte, N. (1995). *Being digital*. New York: Vintage Books.

Newhall, B. (1964). *The history of photography*. New York: Museum of Modern Art.

Shor, I. (1992). *Culture wars: School and society in the conservative restoration 1969–1984*. Chicago: University of Chicago Press.

Sleeter, C. (1996). *Multicultural education as social activism*. Albany: State University of New York Press.

Spring, J. (1986). *The American school 1642–1985*. New York: Longman.

Trow, W. (1963). *Teacher and technology: New designs for learning*. New York: Appleton-Century-Crofts.

7

CYBERBABBLE

A Cautionary Tale About Cyberschools in Pennsylvania

Dominic Scott

Editor's note: Technology's promise of a better approach for life has permeated all aspects of modern society including education. This chapter looks at one experiment with cyberschools and the limitations that were quickly encountered in making the technological miracle come true. This also serves as a cautionary tale regarding the unwarranted expectations of technology from a multicultural education perspective.

Technology's promise of a better way has permeated all aspects of modern society. It is no surprise that it currently enjoys a privileged status in educational discourses. The endless search to make schools more efficient, effective, and exciting finds a ready response from those who believe in technology as a panacea. Postman (1992) refered to this as *technopoly*, "the submission of all forms of cultural life to the sovereignty of technique and technology" (p. 52). He raised it to the status of a metamyth, "with its emphasis on progress without limits, rights without responsibilities, and technology without cost. The technopoly story is without a moral center. It puts in its place efficiency, interest, and economic advance" (p. 179).

Yet at times it seems that the technological revolution going on within schools does indeed hold promise. Computers and the Internet have acted as motivators for many students whose research abilities have been transformed through online access to libraries, museums, and databases. Gorski (2001) acknowledged this when he asserted, "beyond a relatively short learning curve, the resources and materials available via the Internet can expand one's access to new and diverse resources to a virtually infinite degree" (p. 12). However, the availability and access of technological opportunities has been neither smooth nor equitable. The digital divide has mirrored existing disparities of gender, race, ethnicity, class, and educational attainment. For Gorski, the uncritical implementation of technology simply crystallizes already existing inequalities. He asked, "what does it mean that certain racial or ethnic groups enjoy less access to the Internet and its educational opportunities than others?" (p. 15). In their rush to adopt technological innovations, can schools avoid the inherent issues of access and equity that technology brings up? This chapter looks at one experiment with cyberschools and the limitations that were quickly encountered in making the technological miracle come true. It serves as a cautionary tale regarding the unwarranted expectations of technology in the area of schooling of the young.

THE PROMISE OF e-LEARNING

The growth in cyberschools in the United States has been a dramatic and sometimes traumatic phenomenon. Snell (2002) noted, "The 2002–2003 school year marks explosive growth in student enrolment in cyberschools or virtual learning. More than 50 cyber charter schools have launched over the last five years." The belief in the redemptive power of technology to transform student achievement is encapsulated in this claim: "The internet is our best hope for less expensive, more accessible, higher quality education" (Jones, 2002). Such simplistic beliefs in the efficacy of technological delivery of education have lulled many educators into blindly supporting cyberschools. However, the complexities of cybereducation as an effective method of achieving student learning have brought into question this unwarranted optimism. This chapter looks at the impact of Pennsylvania's encounter with cyberschools as an exemplar of how not to implement cybereducation.

Glenn Jones (2002), CEO of Jones Knowledge Inc. and Jones International University, asserted that the "knowledge worker" demands of 21st-century capitalism will ensure a buoyant demand for cyberlearning. The central issue in producing these knowledge workers, according to

Jones, is "how quickly and effectively education can be delivered" (p. xxiii). Indeed the speed and efficiency of this type of knowledge transmission as a contributor to human capital formation is seen as having a greater impact on economic competitiveness in a global market than traditional measures of capital equipment formation. Peppered throughout Jones' book is the belief that cybereducation will create equity and access for the masses "at the lowest cost-worldwide" (Jones, 2002, p. 48). Jones' vision is a rearticulation of the progress myth draped in the mantle of technoefficiency. It comes at a time when traditional U.S. schools are being assailed for failing to produce workers for a global economy and against a backdrop of worldwide scrutiny of public spending on other people's children.

THE HIDDEN CURRICULUM OF E-LEARNING

Jones provided a valuable service in highlighting the attractiveness of cyberschools to cash-strapped state legislatures, transnational corporations, and global investors (the latter of which Jones is a prime example). In 2000, a slew of investment advisories from equity houses Goldman Sachs (2000), Merrill Lynch (2000), and Credit Suisse First Boston (2000) attempted to quantify this potential. Credit Suisse First Boston (2000) foresaw an annual growth rate for e-Learning of 42%, generating a $40 billion market by 2005. Merrill Lynch (2000) estimated an annual growth rate for the K–12 sector of 52%, a $6.9 billion market by 2003. Goldman Sachs (2000) estimated a more modest market size of $2.5 billion by 2003. Goldman Sachs (2000) lamented,

> While distance e-Learning is a large market opportunity, few private companies currently benefit from it. **The overwhelming majority of distance e-Learning is currently provided by two-and four-year public colleges and universities.** These schools also charge low prices for their offerings. (p. 49; boldface original)

This statement should help illuminate corporate America's true interests in e-Learning profits. Clearly, part of the potential for profits in the e-Learning sector comes from the ability to wrest control of distance learning from the colleges and universities and free up the market for higher priced corporate providers. This assault on university monitoring, control, and efficient delivery of distance education is part of a broader campaign to introduce free market policies in the globalized education market.

Cyberschools in particular are being viewed as major components of this globalization process, from both a marketing viewpoint and from a policy perspective. Jones (2002) defined the market for distance learning in global terms:

> Estimates are that distance learning in the United States alone is a $1 billion industry in 2000. That is an increase of more than 100 percent since 1992-93. Worldwide, The distance education market is estimated at $9 billion. When we look at the developing world's need for education, we see that these estimates are just the tip of the iceberg. (p. 111)

However, the pent-up demand for education worldwide will not translate into effective demand in moribund economies, where providing for basic necessities is the major concern of their citizens. Given the dire need of some poor nations, the reallocation of funds from colleges to basic education may actually seem progressive. Desmond (2002) insightfully noted that the equity argument is being proffered by the World Bank and its more recent cousin, the International Finance Corporation, as justification for steering investment away from tertiary education toward basic education. She pointed out that the net effect of this "equity" reallocation conveniently meets the globalization imperative to,

> . . . provide a growing work force of semi-literate, semi-skilled workers for the roving subsidiaries of TNCS [transnational corporations]. Maquilas will be able to find more obedient, more educated workers, more cogs tooled in an educational reform movement that has as its root metaphor, student as worker, and school as commodity. (p. 33)

Once the principle of providing minimal education has been established globally, it is easy to justify the basic provisions as the maximum required from cash-strapped states. This parsimonious logic has been validated by none other than the New York courts when they judged an eighth-grade education as appropriate. "A recent Appellate Division ruling declared that a middle school education in one of New York's lowest performing school districts is all the state constitution guaranteed" (Yinger, 2002). In marked contrast to the 1989 Kentucky Supreme Court decision that defined the state's responsibility to enable students to succeed in academic and competitive job markets, the New York ruling interpreted the state's educational responsibility as marginal:

> This is, of course, a self-fulfilling prophecy. Limiting the state's financial obligation to ensuring the minimal educational standard advocated by this court will relegate a large share of the students in New York City

and other under funded districts to minimum-wage jobs. This standard will also result in citizens with minimal understanding of the complex issues they will confront as jurors and voters. Surely the Empire State can do better than this. (Yinger, 2002)

The neoliberal argument for efficient use of educational funds in less developed countries feeds into pressures to produce semiskilled workers for the new service industries at home. The corporate perspective on cyberschools, both nationally and globally, is of a market-driven, profit-motivated project that co-opts the language of efficiency and equity in the pursuit of profits and market share. Credit Suisse First Boston (2000) encapsulated this sentiment when it asserted that e-Learning companies would generate "superior educational outcomes" while creating "substantial shareholder value."

At a national level, cyberschools complement this search for efficiency, giving hope to those who seek to undermine public schools by redirecting public funding to the presumed more efficient cyberschools. London (2002) pointed out that "on-line schools, freed from geographic boundaries, have entered the competition for students and the tax dollars that follow them." However, this competition has been enabled by state legislatures looking for a quick fix for public education.

LEGAL BASIS FOR CYBERSCHOOLS

The legal basis for cyberschools in Pennsylvania was made possible by the Charter School Law (Act 22) in 1997. Charter schools were first proposed by Albert Shanker, president of the American Federation of Teachers, as far back as 1988. The basic concept was that any group would be able to obtain a charter to run a public school free from some of the bureaucratic limitations of regular public schools. The first charter school began in Minnesota in 1991, and the movement has spread to 36 states, the District of Columbia, and Puerto Rico. This burgeoning in the number of charter schools has been remarkable. As of October 2005, "more than 3,600 charter schools are operating across the United States, serving more than one million children" (Center for Educational Reform, 2006). When Pennsylvania passed the Charter School Law in 1997, few observers saw within it the possibility for cyberschools. However, with the rapidly falling prices of computer workhorses and the abatement of technical glitches in Internet access, creating cyberschools at reasonable costs became feasible and attractive. Although the 1997 law did not expressly prohibit cyberschools, some school districts interpreted the law as a license to create online charter schools (i.e., cyberschools). This reading of the law created tensions and resentment among school boards and ultimately resulted in litigation by the Pennsylvania School Boards Association.

HISTORY OF CYBERSCHOOLS

The first cyberschool was The Florida Virtual School, launched in 1997 to relieve overcrowding in Florida public schools. It quickly blossomed to 10,000 students statewide. The rapid growth of this cyberschool was possible partly because it was entirely state funded and did not depend on school district support. Others quickly followed, and there are now some 50 cyberschools in the United States (Snell, 2002), with somewhat less than 50,000 students (London, 2002). According to Kumar (2002), "of the 25 states that permit cyber charter schools, just two, Pennsylvania and California, have laws specifically dealing with them. Both states implemented legislation as a result of funding and oversight." In fact the Pennsylvanian legislation arose out of the anger and resentment that unregulated and unanticipated cyberschools generated. The Pennsylvania Charter School Law, Act 22, in 1997 allowed any school district in the state to establish charter schools for its students. It did not take long for advocates to realize that charter schools could offer instruction digitally, thus becoming cyberschools. These new cyberschools, although sanctioned by the local school district, were free to operate with considerably more freedom that a traditional public school. Indeed, and they were free to enroll students from any part of the state.

The first cyberschool established in Pennsylvania was the Western Pennsylvania Cyber Charter School, which opened its portals in the 2000-2001 school year. Ironically, this cyberschool was created because the tiny Midland School District "couldn't even find a Pennsylvania school system to take its high school students (they're bussed across the border into Ohio)" (Hardy, 2001, p. 18). However, it was more than local kids who wanted to go to cyberschool. "It was actually a surprise to the school's organizers when it attracted students from across the state, enrolling 525 students from 105 of the state's 501 districts for the 200-01 school year" (Trotter, 2001). But the overnight success of these new cyberschools also brought out the limitations of an unrestricted free market in cyberschooling. Once a student enrolls in a cyberschool in Pennsylvania, his or her home school district is billed for his or her education. Many school districts first became aware of their students attending cyberschools only when the invoices started to arrive. This created immediate problems for school districts. In some cases, school districts had no knowledge of the student in question. In others, the student was still attending a bricks-and-mortar school. In one case, a school district was invoiced for a student who lived in Texas!

Allegations of double dipping and deceit were voiced, and, increasingly, scrutiny of cyberschool accountability was called for. "Some school districts have been billed by more than one cyberschool for a single student. In several cases, invoices have been issued by cyberschools for students who never enrolled in the program" (Pennsylvania School Boards Association, 2001, p. 14).

School boards soon began to question the wisdom of paying for students in unknown programs and of unspecified quality. The required fee for a cyberschool student was 75% of the average per capita cost of educating a child (about $7000), and cyberschools simply invoiced the school district for that amount. Many public school officials contend that cyberschool costs are significantly lower than public school costs, and that transferring 75% of total per capita school costs is simply showering cyberschools with excessive remuneration beyond their true costs. Because cyberschools do not have the overheads of a tradition public school, this arbitrary amount constituted a financial windfall for the cyberschools. Indeed it has been argued that, "by the admission of the cyberschool operators themselves, that figure is many times larger than the cyberschool's actual cost" (Pennsylvania School Boards Association, 2001, p. 4).

A second contradiction in ACT 22 concerns cyberschools in one school district being compensated for students in far-away districts. Not surprisingly, school districts objected to transferring tax dollars to institutions located elsewhere for students they might not even be aware of. For example, the superintendent in Gettysburg, Pennsylvania was reported as saying, "I was being charged on my role in Gettysburg for a student from Dallas Texas" (Kumar, 2002). This brings up the third problem with cyberschools—namely, accountability. This problem is not unique to Pennsylvania. In Ohio, "the cyberschool eCot received $932,030 for 2,270 students [in September, 2000], even though only seven students logged into the cyber class" (Williams, 2002). The naive belief that unregulated charter schools would create a more efficient utilization of public funds was predicated on the notion that innovation, competition, and markets are accountable because of their efficiency.

Accusations of fraudulent billing, broken promises, delays in providing computers and textbooks, special education violations, and shoddy content prompted several school districts to withhold funding. In response, the Pennsylvania Department of Education withheld the full amount of the per child cost of schooling from those school districts. The decision by the then Secretary of Education, Charles Zogby, to support the cyberschools over the public schools might at first seem surprising. However, this action can best be seen as a local manifestation of the ideological agenda for privileging private enterprise over public institutions. In fact an alliance of business interests and conservative public figures was already active in the cyber-school movement in Pennsylvania. For example,

> Virginia-based K12 was founded in 1999 by former U.S. Education Secretary William J. Bennett, and is a subsidiary of the Knowledge Universe Learning Group, an education conglomerate founded by for-mer junk-bond financier Michael Milkin. K12 runs the Pennsylvania Virtual Charter School, one of seven "cyberschools" in the state [of Pennsylvania]. (Brennan, 2002)

It should come as no surprise that, upon his demise as Secretary of Education for the State of Pennsylvania, Charles Zogby took up employ-ment with K12 Inc. Altogether, the Pennsylvania State Department of Education withheld more than $10 million in school funding from school districts in 2002 (Barnes, 2002).

To alleviate concerns about the cost-effectiveness of cyberschools, the Pennsylvania Department of Education contracted KPMG, a consultancy firm, to evaluate the cyberschools. Among its findings were: (a) most cyber-schools did not require parental oversight of students, (b) there were wide variations (20%-80%) in the required time online, (c) most cyberschool stu-dents (56%) had previously been home schooled, (d) only 33% had previ-ously been enrolled in public schools, and (e) several cyberschools were out of compliance with special education law and state standards (PDE Issues Report, 2001). However, the report left many questions unanswered. The biggest cyberschool in the state, the for-profit Einstein Academy Cyber Charter School, accounting for nearly 60% of all cyberschool students, failed to provide comprehensive data to the consultants. Consequently, data emerging from the report were incomplete at best. The report made four major recommendations in the areas of educational accountability, school governance, and financial accountability:

- The Department of Education should look at oversight, approval, and closing of cyberschools.
- Stricter regulations and disclosure should be imposed on new charter schools in the areas of curriculum, state testing, technol-ogy and technology support, privacy, accountability for student authenticity of work, attendance policy and compliance, and delivery of special education services.
- Cyberschools should define the unique qualities of online educa-tion and the responsibilities of parents and students in online education.

- Cyberschools should be monitored to ensure they are interacting with and supporting students and holding them responsible for their educational achievement. (KPMG Consulting, 2001)

However, a growing number of the state's 501 school districts became increasingly concerned with the lack of accountability of cyberschools. Their representative body, the Pennsylvania Schools Board Association, held its own investigation into cyberschools and published its report just weeks before the KPMG report. Of the school districts surveyed, 332 (79%) reported having students enrolled in cyberschools. Some of the major findings of this report were:

- Cyberschool costs primarily are being paid with local tax revenues.
- Only 18% of cyberschool students had been in their districts' regular public schools a year earlier.
- About 6 out of 10 cyberschool students were home schooled in the prior school year.
- Far more than one half of all students in cyberschools are being educated at public expense for the first time—those who previously were home schooled and students who had been in private schools.
- Two cyberschools—the Einstein Academy and the Western Pennsylvania Cyber Charter School—account for nearly 9 out of 10 cyberschool enrollments in 2001–2002.
- Cyberschools lack adequate accountability. (Pennsylvania School Boards Association, 2001, pp. 4-5)

From a multicultural education perspective, two pertinent issues are noteworthy. First is the use of public funds to provide education for previously home-schooled and private-school students. Although private education has received some resources such as transportation and special education services from the public coffers, there has been a careful demarcation between these schools. That only 18% of cyberstudents were in public school the year earlier indicates that the beneficiaries of publicly supported cyberschools were from the private sector. For private- and home-schooled students to benefit from public funds by back-door methods opens up a debate of constitutional proportions. Second, the lack of accountability of cyberschools outlined in the report highlights the responsibility to meet the needs of all students. The representation of special education, minority, and low socioeconomic students must be questioned. Indeed what ideological underpinnings are at work if cyberschools are beyond the standards that public financing requires? Unregulated, cyberschools can quickly become vehicles for resegregation along class, ethnic, and ability lines.

Of the seven cyberschools in Pennsylvania, the Einstein Academy Charter School (TEACH) illustrated the problem of unregulated private cyberschooling. Einstein accounted for more than half of all enrollments in Pennsylvania cyberschools, and it became the focus of much of the contention and criticism of the cyberschool movement (Christopher, 2002). "Opened in the fall of 2001, it admitted more than 3000 students, a number that quickly proved unmanageable" (Kumar, 2002). This was the same cyberschool that allegedly billed the Gettysburg School District for a student from Texas. In January 2001, the Pennsylvania Department of Education filed a lawsuit against Einstein, contending that it was in violation of the Charter School Law and its charter. The Morrisville School District, which granted Einstein's charter, also conducted its own investigation into the charter school. The allegations were: Einstein's offices were not located in the school district that granted the charter (as required by law), special education services were almost nonexistent, the school did not have a psychologist to evaluate special education students, and the central office kept no copies of individual educational programs. (Christopher, 2002).

It seems appropriate to ask, "Whose vision is being implemented here?" Should cyberschools be free to offer education in ways that exclude disabled children, to provide a vehicle for previously home- and private-schooled children to receive cybereducation at public expense, and to enjoy the use of public funds with minimal accountability? K12 Inc., a cyberschool company founded by William Bennett, former Secretary of Education in the Reagan administration, has directly marketed its cyberschools to Christian-based home-schooling associations (Williams, 2002). If this trend continues, cyberschools will have achieved the ultimate neoconservative objective of freeing schools from public scrutiny while they implement an elitist and exclusionary agenda. The vision of publicly funded schools that promote democracy and citizenship by practicing diversity, inclusion, and dialogue will have been violated. The whole case for public-funded schools hinges on the belief that education provides a somewhat level playing field in which even the least advantaged can become everything they can be. To allow public funds to be siphoned off to minimally accountable cyberschools committed to an ideology of the exclusion of students who carry the protection of special education legislation is to engage in a cynical disregard for the law and the democratic urges implied in it.

Another serious allegation was that Tutorbots, the for-profit company that supplied Einstein with curricula, had too cozy a relationship with the school (Einstein offices were housed in a building leased by Tutorbots, one of whose owners was also a founder of Einstein). The Einstein Academy "did not pay teachers for a total of over four months [October through December 2001]. Students received their supplies late, and at one point, Einstein's internet Service provider pulled the plug for overdue bills"

(Kumar, 2002). Einstein, however, did manage to pay Tutorbots about $3 million between September 2001 and January 2002 (Christopher, 2002). "The main thing causing the problem for us is why in the world did Einstein pay Tutorbots $2.3 million when they didn't pay their teachers?" (Lindt, 2002, p. B2), argued John Gould, superintendent of the Morristown School District that granted Einstein's charter. The Pennsylvania Department of Education withheld $3.4 million in funds pending the outcome of the dispute. The lawsuit against Einstein was settled in March 2002, resulting in the school being awarded the $3.4 million in withheld tuition, and the legislature approved a line item of $53 million to reimburse school districts 30% of their cyberschool costs.

Questions remain regarding cyberschools' fulfillment of special education obligations, the definition of what constitutes a cyberschool, and state oversight of cyberschool staffing and standards. Pennsylvania's foray into cyberschools acts as a warning to other states planning to initiate Internet-based instruction. The basic motivation for such schools needs to be questioned, as does their impact on public school financing. Specifically, the quality of instruction and the depth of understanding imparted by cyberschools have not been established. Other innovations in schooling, including the charter school movement as a whole, have failed to deliver on their promise of higher achievement (Toppo, 2002). Can cyberschools deliver or are they simply producing cyberbabble?

CONCLUSION

The Pennsylvania experience with cyberschools offers many lessons for the successful development of this form of instruction. Primarily, the ideological underpinnings of the Pennsylvania cyberschool movement took the form of a defiant attempt to demonstrate that public funds could and should be channeled into educational models that avoid public scrutiny. Even worse, the curricula of these cyberschools were in many cases originated in for-profit enterprises with ideological agendas.

How could it have been done differently? Of the 50 or so cyberschools in the United States, many have worked under or in cooperation with the local school districts. It is no small achievement that Pennsylvania. has managed to transform such harmony and support for educational innovation into such a contentious and litigious squabble. Much of the blame for this must be placed on the open-ended nature of the 1997 Pennsylvania Charter school legislation. The simplistic logic of this legislation seemed to be that a "free" market for educational provision would lead to a more efficient allocation of resources and increase student performance as well.

Nationwide, the charter school movement has not unequivocally demonstrated the soundness of this logic. Of the 2,700 or so charter schools in operation, about 160 have closed for failing to comply with their charter (Center for Educational Reform, 2002). Furthermore, a Brookings Institution report concluded that "charter school students were anywhere from a half year to a full year behind their public school peers" (Toppo, 2002, p. A1).

By attempting to introduce market forces into the public school system (some say to undermine them) the primary vision and mission of the charter school movement was lost. Charter schools throughout the United States define a target population they wish to serve. These are often underserved groups such as inner-city youth, children of color, unique special education populations, or students with special subject area interests. To meet the needs of these unique groups, charter schools attempt to create a specific curriculum, school culture, and teaching strategies tailor-made to fit their needs. In most cases, Pennsylvania cyberschools did not define their mission, other than to be open to all comers. There was no common bond uniting the regular-school, private-school, and home-schooled students other than a desire to learn online.

It is also important to restate that cyberschools are public-funded schools and must exist alongside other public-funded institutions. Cooperation with the public schools is an essential prerequisite for effectively meeting state requirements of reporting, testing, and monitoring students progress and ensuring that students' needs are being met. They must be part of the broader vision of public education while identifying and serving their niche population. Specifically, they must not be allowed to become vehicles for ideological platforms that privilege marketing ideology over scrutiny accountability. If the lessons of 2002 have taught us anything, they have reinforced the need for strict accountability in enterprises predicated on the market metaphor. By creating a market-infused climate in which some cyberschools were able to bill school districts for nonexistent students, students who were still enrolled in public schools, private schools and students who were being home schooled, the Pennsylvania legislation set schools district against school district in a fight to preserve scarce educational tax dollars. By garnishing school district funds when they refused to pay cyberschools for students they did not believe were on the books, the Department of Education demonstrated its ideological bias in favor of cyberschools. Opportunistic use of the Charter School Law enabled school districts to bypass the provision in the law that allowed for regional charter schools that could have provided innovative cybereducation to meet regional needs. This would have fostered cooperation, support, and more efficient use of scarce resources.

Pennsylvania did not have to reinvent the wheel to create effective cyberschools. The Florida Virtual High School, which offers instruction to

10,000 students throughout the state, is entirely state-financed. Supervised by a seven-member board of trustees appointed by the governor, this cyberschool does not compete with public schools, but seeks to supplement them and does not offer diplomas (Kumar, 2002).

The Virtual High School was created for the Hudson Public Schools in Hudson, Massachuettes, in 1996. Now a nonprofit organization, the school works collaboratively with school districts around the country to provide students with courses that are not offered at their home school. More than 200 schools in 24 states and 12 foreign countries, including Spain and Venezuela, participate in the Virtual High School collaborative network. The school employs 167 teachers nationwide. Last spring, more than 2,000 students registered for 134 courses (Joiner, 2002).

This cyberschool "expanded to 3,000 students in 150 high schools across the country" (Gomez & Goodwin, 2001, p. 7). Similar cooperation is evident in the Colorado Online School Consortium, set up specifically to serve home-schooled children, rural, and small schools in Colorado. The importance of collaboration in new technology, curricula, and pedagogy provided the spur for cooperative approaches to cyberschools. The failure of the competitive market-driven model should provide pause for those who see school reform as emanating from the pursuit of selfish interests.

REFERENCES

Barnes, P. (2002, March 15). Cyberschools under fire. *Tech Live*. Retrieved September 17, 2002, from http://www.te4chtv.com

Brennan, C. (2002, November, 27). Zogby said to be in line for job at for-profit schools firm. *Philadelphia Daily News*. Retrieved April 5, 2003, from http://www.philly.com

Center for Educational Reform. (2002, September 17). *Growth in charter schools reflects increasing demands for choices*. CER press release. Retrieved April 6, 2003, from http://edreform.com/press/2002/charternumbers.htm

Center for Educational Reform. (2006, June 6). Charter Schools Highlights. Retrieved June 6, 2006, from http://209.183.221.111/index.cfm?fuseAction = stateStats&pSectionID = 15&cSectionID = 44

Christopher, B. M. (2002, March 20). Judge hears testimony on cyberschool. *The Intelligencer Journal*, pp. A1/A8.

Credit Suisse First Boston. (2000, February 29). *Technology and the internet to change learning in the 21st century*. Retrieved January 31, 2003, from http://www.csfb.com/news/html/2000/february_29a_2000.shtml

Desmond, C. (2002, April 1–5). *The politics of privatization and decentralization in global school reform: The value of equity claims for neoliberalism at the World Bank and in El Salvador*. Paper presented at the annual meeting of the American Educational Research Association, New Orleans, LA.

Goldman Sachs. (2000). *Internet: e-Learning: United States: The birth of a vibrant industry.* New York: Author.

Gorski, P. C. (2001). *Multicultural education and the Internet: Intersections and integrations.* Boston: McGraw-Hill.

Hardy, L. (2001, September). A question of funding: A Pennsylvania case raises concerns about the financing of cyberschools [Electronic version]. *electronic-school.com,* pp. 18-19.

Joiner, L. (2002, September). A virtual tour of virtual schools. Retrieved June 6, 2006, from http://www.asbj.com/specialreports/0902Special%20reports/S5.html

Jones, G. R. (2002). *Cyberschools: An education renaissance.* New York: ibooks.

KPMG Consulting. (2001). *Cyber charter schools review.* Pennsylvania Department of Education.

Kumar, A. (2002, November). Classrooms in the air [Electronic version]. *Governing,* November 2002.

Lindt, S. (2002, March 1). Einstein's charter is in trouble. *The Intelligencer Journal,* pp. B1/B2.

London, H. (2002, September 3). The challenge of cyberschools. Retrieved November 30, 2002, from http:www.washtimes.com

Merrill Lynch. (2000, May 23). *The knowledge web.* New York: Global Fundamental Equities Research Department.

PDE issues report, recommendations on cyberschools. (2001, November). Pennsylvania State Boards Association Information Legislative Service, 39, 1–10.

Pennsylvania School Boards Association. (2001, October). *White paper on cyberschools.* Cumberland, PA: Author.

Postman, N. (1992). *Technopoly: The surrender of culture to technology.* New York: Vintage Books.

Snell, L (2002, October). Cyberschools compete with traditional public schools. *Privatization watch.* Retrieved January 2, 2003, from http://www.rppi.org/cyber schools.html

Toppo, G. (2002, September 3). Charter students test poorly. *The Intelligencer Journal,* pp. A1/A7.

Trotter, A. (2001, October 24). Cyberschools carving out charter niche. Retrieved November 30, 2002, from http://www.edweek.org

Williams, S. (2002). Coming your way: Cyberschools. This newest wrinkle in privatization is being marketed to Christian home-schoolers [Electronic version]. *Rethinking Schools, 16,* 4.

Yinger, J. (2002, August 6). Court leaves thousands of kids behind. Retrieved June 5, 2006, from http://www.cfequity.org/June%2025%20Decision%20Coverage/8-7-02timesunion.htm

8

THE IMPACT OF DOMINANT DISCOURSES ON CULTURAL CONCEPTIONS OF COMPUTERS OF HISPANIC WOMEN

Lizzette M. Rivera

Karen L. Murphy

Editor's note: Currently, technologies are overwhelming the job market and education, influencing public opinion regarding "desires and needs." Many people see how commonplace computers have become and feel that their use is necessary to accomplish work and improve learning. However, the reality is that the media, school, and society-at-large have subconsciously influenced them. This qualitative study explores the cultural impact of computer technologies on 12 economically challenged Hispanic women in an adult literacy program.

Computer technologies are changing how people and institutions communicate, access information, and conduct commerce. Computers supporters and manufacturers assure users that computers and information technologies will make their work easier and faster. Most companies have their own Web site for their customers and suppliers (Futurework, 2000), making buying very convenient from home or the worksite. The charge that "technology is so pervasive in modern times that it is almost inescapable" (Ferré, 1995, p. 9) can be generalized to the presence of computers in society. Supporters argue that computers are a need, not a luxury. The mere presence of computers is a stimulus for a potential customer.

Consequently, it is expected that technological changes bring cultural changes as well. Scardamalia (2000) stated that in the "twenty-first century knowledge work, and technological innovation are inextricably related, as suggested by the global economy. . . . Information-age societies will be founded on new knowledge media and on the redefinition of social and cultural practices afforded by them" (p. 18). Modern technology is influencing culture, demanding a knowledge-based population. Ferré (1995) indicated that we are living in a "technosphere" that is very difficult to avoid. Nevertheless, others believe that it is culture that is changing society to embrace new technologies (Steeter, 2003). As Ellul (1964) indicated, "technology is not a progressive force, but also produces new sociocultural conflicts and uncertainties" (p. 514; cited in Gunkle, 2003).

THEORETICAL BACKGROUND

The mere presence of computer technologies has been impacting the job market and education while influencing how people perceive working and learning. In addition, the mass media, in particular TV and newspapers, provide conflicting messages about advances in computer technologies. Most media messages emphasize that computers bring progress to our lives (e.g., TV reports on the convenience of accessing the Internet from home). Barton (1994) indicated that published advertisements "try to convince readers [in this case viewers] to make these new products part of their lives" (p. 58). Furthermore, such advertising makes some people subconsciously accept "the cultural myth of technology-as-all-powerful-and-good" (Duffelmeyer, 2000, p. 291). Adults typically want the latest electronics on the market; they are convinced they need them even though they did not have them as children.

With the spread of computer technologies in recent decades, people receive positive media messages about the need to adopt new technologies. The messages provide assurance to people that computers will facilitate people's work and children's learning. When parents see these positive messages, they become convinced that computers will help their children "remain competitive in school and in their future careers" (Takayoshi, 1996, p. 199). On the contrary, the media also report negative aspects of computer technologies such as the possibility of the Internet making children more vulnerable to pornography and promising romantic dates that could threaten their personal well-being (Takayoshi, 1996). As a result, individuals also become aware of the negative aspects of computer technologies. However, the positive impact of messages about computers usually outweighs those risks because the pressure of the media promoting the success of computers in education and business is magnified in its influence on people's opinions.

Technologically advanced societies present different messages through the media and society-at-large in positive and occasionally in negative ways. The messages send a subliminal stimulus to viewers or readers (Cooper & Cooper, 2002) through diverse cultural forms. In technologically advanced societies, dominant groups are "able to manufacture dreams and desires" where, without realizing it, people develop common forms of thinking (McLaren, 2003, p. 203). As a result, the impact of the dominant culture is obscured while influencing people's opinions and needs. Dreams and desires can be created subconsciously in individuals who are exposed to positive images of computer technologies that have been promoted as necessary (McLaren, 2003). We are living in the era of a computer revolution "very much like the age of monopoly capital, with new channels of power through which the few try to control both the labor and the leisure of the many" (Ohmann, 1985, p. 684). Ohmann implied that people in power have the ability to develop a demand for products or services for those who need them.

In an ethnocentric society, dominant discourses influence the opinions of minority groups who are subordinate to their norms. Usually, poor minorities with a low education level are more susceptible to this influence. This dynamic is accentuated in the power of the media over consumers, influencing their decisions by using diverse marketing strategies. Media such as TV can reinforce dominant discourses: "Television is the central cultural arm of American society" (Gerbner & Gross, 1976, p. 327; cited in Roberts & Bachen, 1981).

At the beginning of the 21st century, marketing companies began focusing on Hispanic and Latino consumers after the 2000 U.S. Census reported them as the largest minority group surpassing African Americans (U.S. Department of State, 2003). The Hispanic population represents 12.5% (35.3 million) of the total U.S. population. This number does not include Puerto Rico, which adds 4 million more people (U.S. Census Bureau, 2001). Examples of this interest by the private sector are the purchase of Spanish-speaking stations by English-speaking TV stations (Jordan, 2004) and the marketing of products specifically for the taste of the Hispanic market (Wentz, 2003).

Because of the pervasive influence of the media and society-at-large, people's conceptions about computer technologies are socially constructed and impacted by the dominant discourses advocated in their sociocultural context. These adulterated conceptions or opinions become internalized by individuals, and they "appear in a culture as 'natural' and 'normal' because that which is not articulated cannot be argued against nor resisted" (Takayoshi, 1996, p. 198). As a result, individuals perceive computers as important artifacts, necessary in both the workforce and educational environments. Computers, as a dynamic technology, have become a necessary commodity even though they are "unequally distributed therefore differentially accessible" (Bryson & DeCastell, 1998, p. 74).

It was the interest of these researchers to examine selected Hispanic women's cultural conceptions about computer technologies and to determine what factors influence those conceptions.

METHODOLOGY

In an attempt to discover and understand the meanings that participants assign to learning and computers, we selected a qualitative approach. Qualitative research is based on individuals' constructions of reality and their interaction with their social contexts (Merriam & Simpson, 1995) or natural settings (Lincoln & Guba, 1985).

The goal of this study was to understand the cultural conceptions about computer technologies of 12 economically challenged Hispanic women in a family literacy program. We selected a purposeful sampling method because we needed to conduct the investigation with Hispanic women, preferably from low socioeconomic backgrounds. This type of sampling technique is based "on the assumption that the investigator wants to discover, understand, and gain insight and therefore must select a sample from which the most can be learned" (Merriam, 2001, p. 61). Patton (1990) similarly suggested, "purposeful sampling lies in selecting information-rich cases for study in depth. Information rich cases are those from which one can learn a great deal about issues of central importance to the purpose of the research, thus the term purposeful sampling" (p. 169).

This study is part of a broader investigation that examined how selected Hispanic women describe learning and their experience learning computer skills. It also examined how current and past social, historical, and cultural elements influence participants' answers. The data sources used in the main investigation were: (a) Student Background Survey; (b) official records of students; (c) observations of students in the computer class; (d) reflexive journal; (e) interviews with selected teachers; and (f) interviews with selected students. The diverse data sources allowed us to gain a better understanding of the shared culture of the participants.

Context

The study was conducted in the Amigo Family Literacy Program (AFLP), a fictitious name, housed in the Adult Learning Center in a small city in southwestern United States. The center is part of the city school district and is located in a low-income community composed predominantly of Hispanic residents.

The program focuses on low-income parents who have an education need and have children under the age of 8. An important aspect of the program was the provision of child care. As part of the program, the students were enrolled in a 45-minute computer literacy class that met once a week. The primary researcher observed the computer class over a period of 11 weeks, which was the first time that this class had been offered at the center. Changes of instructors, location of the class, and class schedules occurred during the 11 weeks of class observations.

Participants

The participants were drawn from a sample of students enrolled in the AFLP. At the beginning of this study, the program had 26 students, 24 of Mexican origin, 1 African American, and 1 Anglo. Participant selection was a two-stage process: (a) a purposive sample of all the Hispanic students in the AFLP, and (b) a subsample from the same group to be interviewed. Of the 24 Hispanic students, 22 students spoke Spanish as their first language. The age range of the participants was from 16 to 43, with an average age of 28.

Student composition varied during the time of the investigation due to continuous turnover. This turnover presented a challenge for the researchers when following some of the students' stories from the beginning to the end of the study.

Data Source and Analysis

For the purpose of this study, we conducted a series of semistructured interviews with selected students. The interviews allowed us to understand the problem under study from the participants' eyes. Participants narrated their experiences in educational settings and in their personal settings as immigrant adults or native residents. The research question that guided this study was: What are the participants' cultural conceptions about computer technologies?

The primary data source was student interviews with 12 selected students. The students' interview process was performed in three phases (see Table 8.1). Phase 1 was the first interview with 12 purposefully selected students who represented half of the 24 Hispanic students who were in the program at the beginning of the study. This initial interview consisted of seven open-ended questions (see Table 8.2) with prompts for guiding the students in their discussions. Students were selected purposefully for the first interview based on the following factors: (a) responses to the Student Background Survey, (b) teachers' recommendations, (c) data from official records, (d) classroom observations, (e) student's place of origin, (f) attendance, and (g) academic and career goals.

TABLE 8.1
Participants in the Study

Questionnaire + Consent Form (February–March)	Phase 1 First Interview (April–May)	Phase 2 Second Interview (July)	Phase 3 Third Interview (end of July– August)
1. Angie	1. Carmen	1. Carmen	1. Carmen
2. Barbara	2. Cynthia	2. Elba	2. Elba
3. Carmen	3. Elba	3. Irma	3. Mirna
4. Cynthia	4. Elsa	4. Lisa	
5. Elba	5. Gina	5. Miriam	
6. Elsa	6. Irma	6. Mirna	
7. Evelyn	7. Ivette		
8. Gina	8. Lisa		
9. Helga	9. Miriam		
10. Irma	10. Mirna		
11. Ivette	11. Nilsa		
12. Jane	12. Wanda		
13. Lisa			
14. Loren			
15. Mary			
16. Margie			
17. Marianela			
18. Marilet			
19. Maritza			
20. Miriam			
21. Mirna			
22. Nilma			
23. Nilsa			
24. Wanda			

TABLE 8.2
First Interview Protocol With Students

---

1. Tell me about yourself.
2. How has your country of origin helped shape you in terms of who you are today, and why do you think that?
3. What is your opinion about learning?
4. Describe your experience of learning in the Amigo Family Literacy Program.
5. What is it like for you to be learning about computers?
6. How can knowing how to use the computer influence your future?
7. What do you think influenced your opinion about computers?

One of the questions in the first interview, "What do you think influenced your opinion about computers?", provided the basis for this study. After a preliminary analysis of the 12 initial interview transcripts, half of the students were selected for a second interview (Phase 2); of those six students, half were selected for a third interview (Phase 3). The follow-up interviews were more in-depth and customized for each student based on several factors: (a) findings from the first interview, (b) inconclusive issues or unclear responses, (c) changes in the computer class, and (d) particularities of students' stories. Table 8.3 shows the selection process for participants in the three interviews.

The interviews were audiotaped to ensure "that everything said is preserved for analysis" (Merriam, 2001, p. 87) and immediately transcribed. In addition, the primary researcher took notes during each interview, recording interviewee reactions or the importance of statements made by the informants (Merriam, 2001). For English speakers' interviews, it was critical for the primary researcher to record the interviews because English is her second language.

The analysis began with transcribing the interview data. The data were reviewed and categorized according to the emerging themes following the constant comparative method (Strauss & Corbin, 1990). Open coding took place from the raw data during the initial examination of each interview transcript, in which the primary researcher wrote comments and notes in the margins. We did a search of the keywords or phrases of themes in the transcripts, copied the texts, and then pasted them on cards according to preliminary themes found in the literature review. Examples of these themes included computer literacy and the digital divide. From this initial reading of the interviews, the researchers divided the data into categories of information according to the preliminary themes. Emerging themes from subsequent readings of the transcripts were added to the preliminary

TABLE 8.3
Selection Process for Participants in the Interviews

FIRST INTERVIEW	SECOND INTERVIEW	THIRD INTERVIEW
• Responses to the Student Background Survey • Teachers' recommendations • Data found in official records • Personal observations in formal and informal activities • Place of origin (born in United States or Mexico) • Attendance at the comptuer class and learning center • Academic and career goals	• Findings from the first interview (completeness, content, openness) • Student's experience with computer teachers 1 and 2 (due to a change in teachers in the middle of the study) • Attendance at the computer class • Ability to articulate their thoughts • Place of origin	• Essential data for the study (their story, struggles, special abilities, ability to learn goals, family issues, etc.) • Attendance • Availability • Access to a working phone number • Place of origin

themes. After this process, the researchers identified a central category—students' conceptions about computers. Categories and themes were corroborated in the follow-up interviews by member checking (Lincoln & Guba, 1985), which allowed us to verify the data during the study.

Representative comments from the participants are included in the Results section. Pseudonyms were used to maintain anonymity. We established the following method to identify text that is quoted verbatim: Text identification is enclosed in parentheses after the verbatim messages in the text by (I-1), (I-2), or (I-3) to specify Interview 1, 2, or 3.

RESULTS

The results of the research question addressed the cultural conceptions about computer technologies of 12 Hispanic women in a family literacy program. Table 8.4 shows a short history of each interviewee. The results were based on a qualitative analysis of interviews with the participants. Three major findings were that the participants: (a) perceived computers as important and necessary, (b) wanted to gain computer skills to be competitive in the job market and to help their children, and (c) recognized negative and positive aspects of computer technologies.

TABLE 8.4
Students' Short Stories

Carmen

Carmen was born in Mexico, had finished sixth grade, and had been in the program for 1 year and 3 months. She was 27 years old, married, and had one son. Her parents lived in Mexico, but she had relatives in town. Carmen and her family lived in a two-bedroom rental home. She had an old computer that her husband bought for her from her previous boss. Her husband was supportive of Carmen's studies, and for a while he took English classes during the evenings. During the study, Carmen had her computer connected to the Internet. Carmen accessed the Web to do searches for recipes, pictures of Mexico, and learning resources. She also used the computer for basic word processing. She liked crafts and organizing activities and was very outgoing and articulate. Carmen was anxious to learn and was in the advanced English as a Second Language (ESL) class. She attended the computer class regularly. She complained that class was not long enough.

Cynthia

Cynthia was born in Mexico, had finished ninth grade, and had been in the program for only 2 months. She was 22 years old, married, and had a little girl. She was pregnant at the time of the study and stopped coming to the center at the end of the semester. Her parents lived in Mexico. She lived across from the center with her husband, her daughter, and her in-laws in a rental house. At the beginning of the study, she was working in a fast-food restaurant. She did not have a computer and said that she had never used one. She mentioned that she was familiar with computer terms, but "did not remember anything" (I-1). Cynthia's husband did not support her interest in education. At the end of the semester, she came to the primary researcher for advice with this problem, explaining, "I do not have friends; I need someone to talk with." Cynthia was a very quiet, lonely, and passive woman. She was very interested in staying in the program, but her husband was not. She was in the beginning ESL class. She attended the computer class regularly, but had many absences in her other classes.

Elba

Elba was born in Mexico and lived in the United States during her youth. She had a 10th-grade education with some secretarial studies. Elba was 26 years old, divorced, and had three girls. She was the only interviewee living on public assistance. She lived in Title I housing. She reported feeling uncomfortable about being the divorced. Her parents were divorced, and her mother and brother were in Mexico, where they were building a house for her. Her father, however, was in the United States. Elba did not own a computer, but she visited the library and a friend's house to get access to activities for her daughters. She reportedly used the computer for chatting, e-mail, and word processing. Elba was very outgoing, articulate, and positive despite her precarious situation as a single mother. She was in the advanced ESL class. She attended the computer class regularly.

TABLE 8.4
Students' Short Stories *(continued)*

Elsa

Elsa was born in Mexico and had a sixth-grade education. She had been in the program for 9 months. She was 32 years old, married, and had a son and a daughter. Her parents lived and worked in the United States. Elsa lived in a rental mobile home, which was nicely decorated and very clean. At the end of the semester, she was moved from the beginning to the advanced ESL class. She was very happy about that, and her peers congratulated her for that achievement. She reported having a computer, but later discovered that it was not working. Elsa mentioned using the computer for games. She was very insecure learning computer skills and was intimidated by the computer. Elsa reported being a very boring person. She was very quiet, attentive, and motivated to learn. She attended the class regularly and was absent only one time.

Gina

Gina was born in Mexico and had a sixth-grade education. She had been in the program for 4 months. She was 30 years old, married, and had two children. She had lived in the United States for 8 years. Her mother was in Mexico and her father was a seasonal worker in the United States. Gina did not own or have access to a computer. She mentioned that computers are very important to get access to information. Gina reported being very motivated to learn computers because she never had access to one. She had perfect attendance in the computer class, but had many absences in her other classes.

Irma

Irma was born in Mexico and had a sixth-grade education. She had been in the program for 2 years. She was 37 years old, married, and had three daughters. She had lived in the United States for 10 years. Irma lived in a two-bedroom rental mobile home. By the time of the interviews, she had a couple of relatives living with her. Irma bought a $600 used computer for her daughters because she thought they would gain important skills, although she herself was afraid to use the computer. She reported that she had used and accessed a computer before, primarily for games, drawing, and word processing. Irma was in the advanced ESL class and had only one absence in the computer class. Irma was extremely talkative, outgoing, friendly, and very proud of her daughters. She was very motivated to learn and had a great drive to succeed. She reported that she had taken courses in first aid and the first Spanish-language courses in police academy training offered in town.

Ivette

Ivette was born in Mexico. She had finished high school and had taken a business academy course in Mexico. Of the 12 students interviewed, she was only a high school graduate. Ivette was 22 years old, married with children, and lived in a mobile home. She had been in the program for 3 weeks and had arrived from Mexico 5 months previously. Her parents lived in Mexico. Her father, a government employee, was very interested that all his children prepared for careers. Ivette did not own or have access to a computer, but had used one before coming to the center, primarily for games and word processing. She stopped attending the center after the first interview, which took place at the end of the semester.

Lisa

Lisa was born in Mexico and had an eighth-grade education. She had been in the program for 2 years. She was 27 years old, married, and had two children. She married at the age of 15. She and her family lived in a nicely decorated one-bedroom mobile home. Her parents were in Mexico. She had been in the United States 8 years. She did not own or have access to a computer. She reported that she had never used a computer before coming to the center. Although Lisa stopped coming to the computer class, neither the teacher nor the advisor noticed it. This was the reason the researcher selected her for a second interview. She reported that she really liked learning computer skills. She revealed being confused with activities that were scheduled at the same time as her computer class, which was the reason she stopped attending. She also mentioned feeling intimidated by the computer and the fact that some of her classmates knew how to use a computer while she did not. She considered computer skills very important and wished to buy a computer more for the benefit of her sons than for herself. She was in the advanced ESL class. Lisa was a quiet, timid, and reserved person.

Miriam

Miriam was born in Mexico and had a ninth-grade education. She had been in the program for 1 year. She was 33 years old, married, and had three daughters. They had a nice roomy brick home. Her parents were divorced and lived in Mexico. She had knowledge of sales and wanted to open a store in the future. She thought the computer skills she was learning would help to realize that dream. She reported having a computer that she bought at a garage sale, and she had used the computer for educational purposes. She had perfect attendance in the computer class and was in the advanced ESL group. Miriam was an outgoing, friendly, and highly motivated student.

Mirna

Mirna was born in the United States and had a seventh-grade education. She had been in the program for 3 weeks. She was 22 years old, married, and had three daughters. Raised by her grandmother, she reported negative experiences at home. She was a runaway and had her first daughter at age 15. Mirna did not own a computer, but had access to one. Mirna had perfect attendance in the computer class. She was in the GED program and spoke English as her first language. All the teachers said she was a very motivated and self-disciplined student. She was extremely quiet and tended to be isolated from other students, even though she was very open during the interviews.

Nilsa

Nilsa was born in Mexico and had an 11th-grade education. She had been in the program for 1 year. She had taken secretarial studies in Mexico. Nilsa's parents wanted her to pursue a career after high school, but she got married, moved, and did not finish her studies.

TABLE 8.4
Students' Short Stories *(continued)*

Her parents stayed in Mexico. Nilsa lived with her two sons and husband in a mobile home. Nilsa did not own or have access to a computer, but she reported having used one for educational purposes. Nilsa attended the computer class regularly and was absent only one time. She was a close friend of Carmen, and the primary researcher observed how they motivated each other.

Wanda

Wanda was born in Mexico and came to the United States at the age of 13. She dropped out of school in the ninth grade and had been in the program for 9 months. She was 23 years old and married, had three boys, and was living in an apartment. Her parents lived in the United States. Wanda was enrolled in the GED program, and she spoke Spanish as her first language. She was a very disciplined and motivated student. She reported not owning, accessing, or using a computer before coming to the center. Wanda had regular attendance to the computer class, with only one absence. She was extremely quiet and tended to be isolated from other students. It was very difficult to interview her, because most of the time she answered with monosyllables. Wanda found it hard to articulate and share her experiences.

Perception of Computers as Important and Necessary

The first finding is related to the participants' perception that computers are important and necessary. The participants perceived the computer as an integral part of all learning environments. They established a link between learning and computers, considering the computer indispensable to learning or accessing information that would help them learn. They cited as the main reason for needing computer skills the belief that these skills were essential for progress in their present U.S. culture. Although many of the participants did not own or use a computer, they assumed that computer skills would help them and their children to acquire learning and to succeed in school, and for that reason these skills were perceived as very important.

Most students mentioned that they would like to own a computer and have access to the Internet. Some students owned or had used a computer, but they used it only for basic applications such as painting, drawing, word processing, and games. Students perceived a need to possess computer skills. For example, Irma said, "Now almost everything needs to be on computers or by the Internet, everything. I think that, yes, we need to learn computers. It is a good thing for us" (I-2). Earlier, Irma had bought a $600 used computer for her daughters. Irma explained that she never used the computer because she was afraid to break it, but she ensured that her daughters knew how to use it. Participants like Irma are convinced that computer skills are important. The participants accessed or observed computers in the learning center and at their children's schools.

Of all of the students interviewed, Carmen demonstrated the greatest interest in teaching herself. Curiously, with only a sixth-grade education, Carmen learned to access the Internet after her husband bought an old computer for her. One of her favorite activities was searching for recipes. Carmen would first enter the Univision Web site, the Spanish TV network, and from there she accessed other Web sites. Carmen explained that she also "logged into the Internet to learn English. When I need information, I access a Web site where I can post my questions" (I-1). On one occasion, she posted a question about finding a program where she could learn English and subsequently received a program to learn English, written in English and Spanish, in the mail.

Computers were one of the resources needed in the participants' current learning environment in the United States. Because participants noticed the presence of computers in places that they usually visited (e.g., medical and social services, schools, and utility offices), they generalized that computers are necessary in any work environment. Participants stated this as an important reason that they and their children needed to learn computer skills. Students cited the importance of computers to succeed in school and the workplace, and for their children's futures. Some, however, recognized that they had other financial priorities and could not afford to buy a new computer. As Elba explained, "There are many Hispanics who struggle to have something good in their lives. They are probably interested in computers, but sometimes we have . . . , at least I have, other priorities. There are other things first. I would like to have a computer, but it is a luxury for me, something that I really do not need" (I-1).

Participants' opinions about computers were influenced by other factors in their daily lives: the visual media. Television influenced participants' conceptions about computers. When participants watched TV commercials and news reports about computer technologies, they stated that they would like to own a computer and felt motivated to learn computer skills. As McLaren (2003) implied, people perceive a need for a computer, and they want to have the artifact that they see on TV. External forces such as TV and the learning center drove the participants' needs and desires for computers.

Interest in Gaining Computer Skills

The second finding is that the participants wanted to gain computer skills to be competitive in the job market and to help their children.

Competing in the Job Market. As mentioned earlier, students thought that computer skills are essential for the working environment because they observed computers in the offices that they visited. Students generalized by saying that computers are everywhere and assumed that being computer literate would open the doors for the job market. Cynthia explained, "You find computers in every place and find a better job if you know computers, because stores and all types of jobs have computers" (I-1). Cynthia thought that Hispanics would be more competitive in the job market if they knew about computers. Irma explained, "In the church that I attend, all the paperwork is done using computers. They needed a secretary and asked me, but I told them that I did not know too much computers yet, just the first steps" (I-1). She emphasized that she always told her daughters of the importance of learning to use computers to be better prepared for the job market, and that is the reason she bought one for them. Irma lived with her three daughters and husband in an old two-bedroom mobile home; their family struggled because only her husband worked and, like most of the interviewees' husbands, in a low-income job. However, she perceived that the computer was important. Irma explained, "I have a computer. I do not use it; I do not want to break it. My daughters are the ones who use the computer. They take classes in the school, and learn everything faster" (I-1).

Helping Their Children. Like most parents, participants were worried about the well-being of their children and being able to prepare them for the future. The participants perceived computer skills as necessary for the progress of their children. They believed that if their children possessed computer skills, they would have better chances in school and later in the job market. Cynthia, Gina, Irma, and Miriam shared that if their children learned computer skills, they would be better equipped for the future workforce.

In addition, participants emphasized their preoccupation with being able to answer their children's questions about computers. As Elba explained, "when they [children] come and say something about computers, you do not react with 'what are you talking about?' . . . If we know about computers, we can tell our children and help them to progress in life" (I-2). Elsa commented similarly on the value of becoming computer-literate: "When they learn in school how to use a computer, I will be familiar with what they are doing. In that way, I understand more what my children are doing with the computer" (I-1).

Students not only wanted to learn computers, but also wanted to improve their English skills because of their children. They believed that with computer skills, along with improved English skills, they would be able to help their children with homework. Most of the students stated that learning English was their primary motivation for enrolling in the literacy program. When they discovered that they could also take computer classes, they became very enthusiastic and even more motivated, an "unexpected surprise" according to Elba (I-2).

Most of the mothers were aware that their children were learning computers skills in school, and they spoke of their motivation to learn computers to help their children with their homework. Carmen mentioned several times her interest in helping her toddler son in the future. She explained, "I could help my child with his homework, because there will be many assignments on the computer. I am very interested in being able to help my son if he asks, 'Mother, help me'" (I-2). Carmen was the most motivated and fastest learner in both the English and computer classes.

Recognition of Negative and Positive Aspects of Computer Technologies

The third finding is that the participants recognized negative and positive aspects of computer technologies. Participants paid special attention to the development of computer technologies, but more specifically to the reports of the benefits and dangers of the Internet. These reports were presented on TV documentaries, which detailed cases of child pornography and risks of online relationships. Although the researchers had not considered this finding during the design of the investigation, it was raised by most of the participants during the interviews. They had basic knowledge of what the Internet is and how it can be used. When they heard the TV news, they feared that their children might become involved in such "negative" experiences (Elba, I-1). In addition, participants reported a great distrust of relationships generated online. Students cited TV news alerting people about the risks of online relationships that can lead to crime. Lisa was aware of these issues, although she did not own or had not used computers before. She was informed of the potential for the Internet to be a corrupting influence on minors, as she explained, "girls meet boyfriends through the computer and it can really be a trap for them" (I-1). Nilsa stated another concern about the negative impact of the Internet on children: "Many people say that on the computer you can learn how to make a bomb" (I-1). Similarly, Gina was afraid of the negative influence of the Internet and information that children can access. She said, "The only thing that I do not like about computers is that children can see dirty things on the Internet" (I-1). The participants' negative comments were very similar with access to pornography on the Internet as their main concern. Because of the events they heard on the news, many parents were overprotective with their children; two of them reported not allowing their children to visit their friends' houses by themselves.

On the positive side, participants recognized the advantages of the computer and the Internet. Carmen searched for recipes, information about Mexico, and resources to learn English. Elba visited the library with her daughters to access the Public Broadcasting Station (PBS) Web site. She liked her daughters' experience with online games and coloring books. Irma explained to her daughters the magnificent special effects on TV and movies using computers and specialized software. She encouraged her girls to learn computers and pursue a career where they could have a good income working "just with a click of a button" (I-1). She explained to her daughters the importance of pursuing a career to avoid falling into dead-end jobs where they would need to work all day in the sun like their father.

The students were aware of the uses of computer technologies. For example, Mirna was aware of how easily information can be sent using e-mails "from one place to another instead of using the telephone" (I-1). She also believed that computers would help her to improve her reading and writing skills, areas in which she was working very hard. She was trying to pass the General Educational Development (GED) examination, having only finished eighth grade. Other uses mentioned by students such as Miriam were that computers can be used to store information and that information can be retrieved when needed. Miriam hoped to open her own business in the future, and she planned to use a computer to manage her business.

Participants were aware of the positive and negative aspects of computer technologies, but the positive prevailed over the negative. Those students who did not own a computer voiced their interest in having one, but they explained that buying a computer did not fit into their immediate financial priorities. As Lisa explained to her older son, "with the money that I need to buy a new computer, I can save it for the down payment on a house" (I-2). Lisa and her family rented a one-bedroom house; one of her wishes for the future was to buy a home of their own, but she also expressed her desire to buy a computer for her son.

In summary, the results of this qualitative study showed that Hispanic female students enrolled in this computer literacy class: (a) perceived computers as important and necessary, (b) wanted to gain computer skills to be competitive in the job market and to help their children, and (c) recognized the negative and positive aspects of computer technologies.

CONCLUSIONS AND IMPLICATIONS

Mexican Women's Cultural Conceptions About Computers Technologies

The results of this qualitative study indicated that the 11 Mexican women and 1 Mexican-American woman demonstrated that, although most of them had no previous experience using computers, they showed a positive attitude toward them and perceived computers as important and necessary for their academic and career futures. They also recognized such positive aspects of computer technologies as the capabilities of the Internet as a source of information and the negative aspects of computer technologies as the potential dangers of the Internet.

The results support findings of other scholars who suggest that people's conceptions are socially constructed and impacted by the dominant culture through different entities of society. What entities and experiences helped to shape participants' conceptions? The findings of this study reveal several factors that shaped or influenced participants' conceptions about computer technologies: (a) lived experiences, (b) personal struggles, (c) visits and observations to other people's work, (d) the adult literacy center, (e) children's experiences in the school, (f) teachers and friends, and (g) print and visual media. The results of this investigation further indicate that society, school, and the media influenced participants' cultural conceptions of computer technologies.

The Society

Although most of the participants had a minimal level of education and lived in low-income housing, they recognized the impact of computers and the Internet on their current society. For example, participants were aware of the information they could access on the Internet about cooking recipes, health issues, learning English, and activities for their children.

When people in poverty face this overwhelming promotion of technologies in society, they are likely to become aware of being computer-illiterate. They may decide to buy a computer or enroll in classes hoping to learn and become computer-literate. Selfe (1999) pointed out that some ethnic groups "continue to have less access to high-tech educational opportunities" (p. 423), making them less computer-literate and decreasing their share in diverse computer-related jobs. The present study focused on 12 females of Mexican heritage enrolled in a computer class in a family literacy program. Of the 12 students, 11 were born and raised in Mexico, and 1 student was a third-generation Mexican American. All of the participants were living at the poverty level, the main reason that they were accepted into the family literacy program. Therefore, when compared with other groups in society, the students in this program were at an academic and economic disadvantage.

The School

Students enrolled in the family literacy program to learn English or obtain their GED. The Mexican participants who had recently immigrated to this country felt that they would be better able to integrate into this culture if they could communicate effectively in English. By enrolling in the program, participants demonstrated a high level of commitment to the needs of their children, which was their main motivation. They also felt honored and recognized when they were accepted into the literacy program because it has a high rate of applications. After students were part of the program, they were bombarded with messages about the importance of learning English and earning their GED. All students mentioned one or both reasons as their main goals in the program.

The computer class opened a new window for the students' future, and they felt those skills would help them when their children ask questions about computers. As Miriam explained, "these classes that we are having in the center may be the only opportunity for most of us to learn how to use computers" (I-2). Participants were hopeful about the future of the computer class in which they were enrolled.

The Media

Hispanics are the fastest growing minority group. Recent population estimates show that Hispanics comprise 13% of the total population, making them the main minority group in the United States (U.S. Census Bureau, 2003). All 12 Mexican women interviewed lived on limited budgets. Their husbands worked in low-level and low-paying jobs. For many families in poverty, TV is their main source of information. Media research suggests that more families prefer to own a TV than a telephone (Nielsen Media Research, 1995). These factors—living in poverty and relying on TV— seemed to influence the participants' perceptions by causing them to develop adulterated cultural conceptions about the need and desire for computer technologies.

As cited by most of the students, the visual media provided knowledge about issues related to computer technologies. They watched TV reports about computers and mentally translated the messages based on their current context (Hall, 1974). In the United States, the use of computers is highly promoted, and computer skills are perceived as essential. Participants assumed that computers were necessary and stated their desire to buy one. The participants' cultural conceptions about computers and the Internet were consistent with the messages received from the media. From TV reports, viewers perceived computer advances as omnipotent elements in education and the job market, and they assumed that those advances would improve their learning. McLaren (2003) explained this phenomenon as the dominant culture trying "to 'fix' the meaning of signs, symbols, and representations to provide a 'common' worldview, disguising relations of power and privilege through the organs of mass media" (p. 203). In short, the media promote computer technologies as a symbol of economic progress.

FINAL THOUGHTS

Many of the women demonstrated a great commitment to the computer class and recognized the importance of having computer skills. They conveyed their interest in having the class last more than 45 minutes or be offered more frequently. They also shared their concerns about the future of the class, improvement of facilities, and having a permanent computer teacher. The participants shared their feelings of being honored to participate in this study.

During the computer class, most of the Hispanic women participants saw the primary researcher, who is bilingual in English and Spanish, as another teacher, and they felt comfortable asking her questions in their native language. However, this practice represented a dilemma to the primary researcher in determining the level of involvement she should have in the computer class and with the students. Outside the classroom, the participants saw the researcher as a friend and shared with her many dreams, advice, and their experiences in this country. This phenomenon, reported in the literature as an ethical consideration in data collection, is typical during interviews that may improve the condition of participants (Merriam, 2001). We appreciate all the Hispanic women who kindly participated in this investigation. We recognize their motivation to improve as human beings, their roles as responsible parents, and their commitment to learning.

REFERENCES

Barton, E. L. (1994). Interpreting the discourses of technology. In C. L. Selfe & S. Hilligoss (Eds.), *Literacy and computers: The complications of teaching and learn-*

ing with technology (pp. 56-75). New York: The Modern Language Association of America.

Bryson, M., & DeCastell, S. (1998). Telling tales out of school: Modernism, critical, and postmodern "true stories" about educational computing. In H. Bromley & M. W. Apple (Eds.), *Education/technology/power: Educational computing as a social practice* (pp. 65-84). Albany: State University of New York Press.

Cooper, J., & Cooper, G. (2002, November). Subliminal motivation: A story revisited. *Journal of Applied Social Psychology, 32*(11), 2213-2228.

Duffelmeyer, B. B. (2000). Critical computer literacy: Computers in first-year composition as topic and environment. *Computers and Composition 17*, 289-307.

Ferré, F. (1995). *Philosophy of technology*. Athens: The University of Georgia Press.

Futurework: Trends and challenges for work in the 21st century. (2000, Summer). *Occupational Outlook Quarterly, 44*(2), 31-36.

Gunkle, D. J. (2003). Second thoughts: Toward a critique of the digital divide. *New Media & Society, 5*(4), 499-522.

Hall, S. (1974). The television discourse—encoding and decoding. In A. Gray & J. McGuigan (Eds.), *Studies in culture: An introductory reader* (pp. 28-34). London: Arnold.

Jordan, M. (2004, April 15). Telemundo network takes on Univision with help from NBC. *Wall Street Journal*, p. B.1.

Lincoln, Y. S., & Guba, E. G. (1985). *Naturalistic inquiry*. Newbury Park, CA: Sage.

McLaren, P. (2003). *Life in schools: An introduction to critical pedagogy in the foundations of education* (4th ed.). Boston: Pearson.

Merriam, S. B. (2001). *Qualitative research and case study applications in education: Revised and expanded from case study research in education*. San Francisco, CA: Jossey-Bass.

Merriam, S. B., & Simpson, E. L. (1995). *A guide to research for teachers and trainers of adults* (2nd ed.). Malabar, FL: Krieger.

Nielsen Media Research. (1995). *Report on television*. Palo Alto, CA: Author.

Ohmann, R. (1985, November). Literacy, technology, and monopoly capital. *College English, 47*(7), 675-689.

Patton, M. Q. (1990). *Qualitative evaluation and research methods* (2nd ed.). Newbury Park, CA: Sage.

Roberts, D. F., & Bachen, C. M. (1981, January). Mass communication effects. *Annual Review of Psychology, 32*, 307-356.

Scardamalia, M. (2000, November 21–24). *Social and technological innovations for a knowledge society*. International Conference on Computers in Education/International Conference on Computer Assisted Instruction, Taipei, Taiwan. (ERIC Document Reproduction Services No. ED 454 814)

Selfe, C. L. (1999). Technology and literacy: A story about the perils of not paying attention. *College Composition & Communication, 50*(3), 411-436.

Steeter, T. (2003, September). The romantic self and the politics of internet commercialization. *Cultural Studies, 17*(5), 648-660.

Strauss, A., & Corbin, J. (1990). *Basics of qualitative research: Grounded theory procedures and techniques*. Newbury Park, CA: Sage.

Takayoshi, P. (1996, October). Writing the culture of computers: Students as technology critics in cultural studies classes. *Teaching English in the Two-Year College, 23*(3), 198-204.

U.S. Census Bureau. (2001, May). *The Hispanic population: Census 2000 brief.* Retrieved June 18, 2004, from http://www.census.gov/prod/2001pubs/c2kbr01-3.pdf

U.S. Census Bureau. (2003, February). The foreign-born population in the United States: March 2002, population characteristics. *Current Population Reports.*

U.S. Department of State. (2003, January 23). *Hispanics replace African Americans as largest U.S. minority group* [International Information Programs]. Retrieved August 15, 2004, from http://usinfo.state.gov/usa/diversity/a012303.htm

Wentz, L. (2003, July 7). Pepsi puts interests before ethnicity. *Advertising Age, 74*(27), p. S4.

9

DEVELOPING A MULTICULTURAL DISCOURSE WITH PRESERVICE TEACHERS USING DISCUSSION BOARDS

Julie Horton

Editor's note: This chapter investigates students' development in the area of multicultural education utilizing discussion boards. Students were asked to enhance and continue the discussions beyond the boundaries of class meeting times. Horton challenged her students to study the impact of race, ethnicity, class, language, gender, sexuality, and exceptionality on education. An analysis of the online journals is shared to examine the use of technology in this process.

The purpose of this chapter is to investigate the development of preservice teachers' discourse in the area of multicultural education. It was hoped that these students would develop a discourse of their own and ultimately use this in their future classroom practices. During the 2002 Spring semester, a new course was implemented in an elementary education program entitled *Learner Diversity*. In this course, students were asked to explore "current literature and practices related to issues of learner development, exceptionalities, and cultural diversity" (Horton, 2002). As a distance education course, discussion boards were utilized to facilitate this process.

The first part of this chapter illustrates the preservice teachers' investigation into their own identity through readings and activities. Many multicultural educators believe that teachers cannot possibly begin to understand other cultures until they begin to unpack the complexities surrounding themselves (Banks, 2003; Dilg, 1999; Helms, 1993). The second half of the chapter shares a selection of student work through online journaling related to issues of race, class, and language. These journals illustrate the personal frustration and angst that this work involves. Technology has been seen by many as a "quick fix" for our many problems in society. Did the use of technology assist in this process? Were the students able to fully communicate with each other or did it hinder their process and development?

CONTEXT

This teacher education program is situated in a rural mountain region on the east coast of the United States. The university, nestled in the Appalachian Mountains, serves a student population that is primarily White (92.3%) and tends to come from a middle- to upper-class background (Williams, 2003). Unique to the situation of the Spring 2002 was the fact that this particular course was offered to a cohort as part of an extension program—what those in this area term *off-the-mountain*. Therefore, the students came from a completely different background than those on campus. Although still located in the Appalachians, most of the students were in their second career, had started families, and were not as privileged as those attending classes on campus.

The course, *Learner Diversity,* that framed this chapter was offered as part of a new elementary education program. The goals of the *Learner Diversity* course included:

1. Articulate how student learning is influenced by individual experiences, talents, and prior learning, as well as development, language, culture, family, and community.
2. Develop insights into how their own cultural and family backgrounds influence the way they view their students and schools.
3. Develop an understanding of cultural diversity and how to incorporate multicultural experiences into instruction.
4. Begin to develop a wide repertoire of teaching strategies to promote each child's learning and development in an appropriate, inclusive environment.
5. Develop an understanding of areas of exceptionalities in learning, including talented, and gifted and special needs, and how to access strategies to accommodate individual differences.

6. Develop the ability to use cultural diversity and individual stu-   ˙
    dent experiences to enrich instruction.
7. Develop a greater understanding of the importance of accepting
    and valuing all students from different cultures and fostering
    equitable treatment of those students.

This crucial class encompasses and exposes preservice teachers to issues such as race, ethnicity, language, socioeconomic status (SES), sexual orientation, gender, exceptionalities, and religion. The practicum provides students with grounding for working with a diverse population as well.

REVIEW OF LITERATURE

Multicultural education should be used in any classroom as a tool to support the development of identity and critical thinking. It can educate teachers and students who will grow up to make deep and lasting changes in the basic structures of society (Ramsey, 1998). However, these lofty goals cannot be attained until the teachers are able to work with children at all levels. Stuart and Thurlow (2000) reported that preservice teachers' beliefs and understandings of multicultural education tended to be superficial. According to an initial survey conducted at the beginning of the semester, the majority of the responses asking for a definition for multicultural education included an awareness of or exposure to other cultures. Rather than viewing multicultural education as an entire "frame of mind" for life or a framework for education, this could be achieved by celebrating a holiday or mentioning an accomplishment of a minority. Teachers may not realize that this, but by teaching in this way, students are actually degrading an entire culture (Banks, 2003).

Stemming from the literature of the 1990s, the personal identity of teachers is a crucial issue that cannot be ignored. Teachers cannot possibly begin to understand other cultures until they begin to understand their own identity (Banks, 2003; Goodwin, 1994; Greenman & Kemmel, 1995; Rodriguez, 1993). A teacher's cultural identity has a direct impact on the instruction and learning environment in any classroom. Zeichner and Liston (1996) echoed this sentiment; "In order to understand and direct our educational practice, we need to understand our own beliefs and understandings . . . [because] so much of teaching is rooted in who we are and how we perceive the world" (p. 23). Unchanged is the fact that teachers continue to predominantly emerge from a White, middle-class, homogeneous background that is mostly different from that of the student population (Clark & O'Donnell, 1999; Irvine & Armento, 2001; New, 1995; RCOE,

2000). As a result, they often bring the beliefs and values of this group with them into the classroom.

Significant to this, is the tendency for White people to perceive themselves through a transparent lens in which Whites do not consider their personal behaviors, or views as being the 'standard' mainly because they never had to (López, 1996). This serves as the basis for being privileged in U.S. society that are rarely "fully acknowledged, lessoned or ended" (McIntosh, 1989, p. 10). For Whites, the process of identity development involves becoming aware of one's "Whiteness," accepting this aspect as socially meaningful, and internalizing a positive view of Whiteness not based on superiority. Thus, racial identity development refers "to the belief systems that evolve in response to the racial group categorizations given by society" (Tatum, 1999, p. 57).

Once teachers have come to grips with their own personal compartmentalization of "others," they can begin to work toward adapting a culturally responsive classroom practice for their own classroom (Larkin, 1995). Avoiding ethnocentric explanations of students' behavior, teachers must be mindful not to interpret behavior from their own culturally biased viewpoints. This is a constant struggle. Thus, institutions of higher education must support our teachers in this journey toward an equitable education for all students.

Teachers must also be willing to honestly and openly discuss "their own feelings, values and attitudes relating to race, class, gender and other difficult dimensions of multicultural teaching" (Ladson-Billings, 1994, p. 5). Unless teacher educators begin questioning their students in terms of personal identity, beliefs, and values, this writer believes that traditional teaching practices will continue. When teachers fail to challenge the status quo (such as their own perceptions, attitudes, and assumptions about children), inequities can arise in the classroom that is soon accepted as unavoidable (King, 1991; Ladson-Billings, 1994).

One example of a negative outcome of traditional teaching practices may be seen in the persistent, pervasive, and disproportionate school failure among Chicanos (Valencia, 1991). Although Valencia gives several causes for this, including continued segregation, language/cultural exclusion, and lack of school financing, teachers also play a large role (Connell, 1994). Teachers' perceptions of Chicano students may be discriminatory in their education (Lima & Lima, 1998). For example, teachers may have beliefs that Chicano students have lower IQs, and are thus inferior to Anglo students. This in turn affects curriculum, special education placement, and poor teacher–student interactions (Quintanar-Sarellana, 1997; Retish & Kavanaugh, 1992; Valencia, 1991).

For the opportunity gap to narrow, Houser (1996), asserted that teachers must modify their beliefs and attitudes that continue to perpetuate the situation. A teacher must work on self-development, rather than just cultural awareness, to become a multicultural person. This is a continual struggle in that "the search for identity always entails the confrontation of unpleasant truths about our individual and collective past" (Buckley, 2000, p. 51). Teachers must now take responsibility for their influence in the educational system for real change to occur in the classroom.

METHODOLOGY

Because the purpose of this inquiry was to assist student teachers in the development of their own multicultural views and practices in the classroom, the first step was to ascertain where the student teachers were in their own growth through informal surveys taken at the beginning of class. The second step of the study was accomplished through online journaling throughout the class, in which students were able to dialogue with the instructor and other students about readings and the classroom discussion. This opened up another avenue for further dialogue that appeared to encourage many students. Online communication provided some students with a sense of anonymity. This communication style allowed some students the opportunity to voice their opinions more often and some said more online than they did in class. This also allowed our discussions to continue long after each class had ended.

The 20 participants in this study were part of an elementary education co-hort of an off-campus extension program. Nineteen were female and one was male. All were White and admittedly came from a lower to working-class, conservative, Southern Baptist background. Their journals were completed online after class. The use of on-line journaling was twofold. First, the journals were utilized to continue discussions curt short due to the time constraints of meeting once a week. Because this was an extension class, there were particularly bad weather conditions, and the 20 students lived in nine surrounding counties, the journals were particularly useful. Second, the journals fostered substantive thought and engaged students in their learning (Hay, 2003). This was a Web-assisted classroom, and the journaling enhanced our distance. This route did include extra work on the part of the professor, but it also extended the discussion in ways impossible before.

On the completion of the semester course and after grades had been posted, data analysis began. Data analysis is the cyclical process of systematically searching and arranging all of the data, including the initial surveys, personal notes, and online journals, searching for patterns to discover what has been learned (Bogdan & Biklen, 1998; Goetz & LeCompte, 1984; Spradley, 1979). The data continue to be revisited today as the researcher is able to make new connections and understandings with the literature and data (Emerson et al., 1998). This is why the data had to be revisited periodically as understanding evolved with new information altering the existing coding system.

DISCUSSION

Because all of these preservice teachers fall into this category, this teacher educator focused heavily on White identity development. As discussed earlier in this chapter, the majority of these students viewed multiculturalism in a very superficial light, such as "bringing in another culture," or being "open-minded." For the purposes of this chapter, two students' online journal excerpts were used to illustrate their growth.

As data analysis continued, the themes that emerged were powerlessness and anger:

> Hatred is not a good thing, and as education professionals it will be up to us not to tolerate it in our classrooms. But how can we do this? Almost daily I will have a student come to me to tell me that he/she cannot sit next to so-and-so. Generally I ignore this and tell the student to get over it—that we must all learn to live and work together. (Student A: 1/20)

This teacher's aide appears powerless to assist students and talked about how there was nothing she could do to help kids—that it was just a way of life. It appeared as if she were saying, "Kids will pick on kids. That's just the way it is." In class she did not see the point to making a big deal about the color of anyone's skin. The next entry demonstrates the extreme anger and defensiveness projected in the classroom for the first 6 weeks of class:

> After I read chapter three I was very irritated! I was on the defense. I even answered one of the discussion questions in a cynical way. I wrote that immigrants also migrated to the United States to learn about specific aspects of our culture and then use their knowledge to kill us. (Student D: 1/31)

This student was responding to a class reading involving racial history in the United States. She jumped immediately to the defensive side as did many of her colleagues. This continued and I soon wondered about disbanding the online journal because it seemed a place for adding fuel to the fire, but this changed in mid-March.

> After I watched the Shadow of Hate video, my agitation turned to shame. The book makes us out to be monsters and that irritated me. . . . The video confirmed that the dominant culture that we are associated with was and still is a monster. The video gave me a better understanding as to why certain cultural groups have issues with the dominant culture. I can erase the past by educating the future. . . . (Student D: 3/3)

Even the teacher's aide who seemed powerless before was now speaking about incorporating all cultures and "not just the regular basic white male education," which appeared a step in the right direction (Student A: 3/3 Journal). At least now Student A was viewing herself as part of the solution and not a helpless participant in the school. I believe Student A's hesitation came from her own experience. She shared this in her journal:

> As I watched the video I had a lot of strong feelings. My best friend's great great grandmother accused an African American man in this area of raping her because she was afraid because his family had moved close to hers. This fear is what drives so much of the hatred in our society. This fear of the unknown and of what is different to us. I thought it was just ignorant people expressing themselves in even more ignorant ways. (Student A: 3/4)

By the end of the course, it appeared that students began to at least harness the courage to look outside their beginning beliefs of diversity. Not everyone had changed, but most were at least willing to listen and incorporate differing ideas in the classroom.

> We live in an ever-changing society and as future educators we have a huge responsibility ahead of us. . . . We must set aside any underlying stereotypes or prejudices we might have and get to know our students as the person they really are not the students we expect them to be. (Student D: 4/27)

> I believe as teachers it is our responsibility to help expose students to different cultures, races, religions, etc. (Student A: 4/24)

CONCLUSIONS

In terms of students' initial definitions of multicultural education, the findings were similar to the literature, demonstrating that students tended to view multicultural education from a minimalist or simplistic perspective (Grant & Koskela, 1986; McCarthy, 1994). By the end of the class, 16 of the 20 students felt that children should be exposed to diversity, but the means by which to do so differed by the specific issue involved. Although many students seemed comfortable about discussing issues of class and gender, some still felt that race "had been done to death" and "Blacks should just get over it." Also, a majority of students did not feel that religion or sexuality should be dealt with in the schools. These were "sacred" subjects, as one student put it, and should be left up to the home. In her final journal, one student wrote that a teacher should teach the "right" morals and not have to be accepting of everyone else. "What about our rights?", another student asked.

However, all of the preservice teachers struggled in the actual practice of their definitions during their internships. This leads the researcher to believe that students need more than just a single course in multicultural education. Preservice teachers must view multicultural education in practice throughout all of their methods classes.

There also appeared to be differed levels of discourse patterns of multiculturalism. One level (where the majority of preservice teachers left the class at) leads children to tolerance and empathy, whereas the other incorporated diversity as "a way of life" and used it as a teaching tool. The ultimate goal of a teacher education program should be to "interrupt, challenge and change the ways teachers think about themselves and 'others'" (Gomez, 1994, p. 14). The next step in this process is to inquire how effectively new teachers are able to implement curricula, strategies, and skills into their own classrooms. This suggests that there should be a support system in place to assist new teachers as they move into their future careers and to strengthen the professional development of teachers already out in the field.

McCarthy (1994) suggested that, "the elimination of prejudice through exposing white teachers and students to sensitivity training has not produced the intended result of prejudicelessness" (p. 88). Other research, including this small study, points out that prior experiences can be more powerful than simply reading a multicultural text. Therefore, teacher educators must be mindful to engage students in a sustained examination of the complex practices involved in the social, political, and theoretical arenas of schooling practices (McCarthy, 1994).

It is vital that all teachers are able to teach to diverse populations because it is becoming apparent that most will be doing just that. This means that a program of multicultural teacher education must be developed so that all students receive an equal educational opportunity and not one that dictates the values, identities, and cultures of one over another. This research adds to the literature on multicultural education by studying the development of discourse in the classroom that ultimately leads to practice.

REFERENCES

Banks, J. A. (2003). Multicultural education: Historical development, dimensions, and practice. In J. A. Banks & C. A. McGee Banks (Eds.), *Handbook of research on multicultural education* (pp. 3-24). New York: Simon & Schuster.

Bogdan, R. C., & Biklen, S. K. (1998). *Qualitative research in education: An introduction to theory and methods.* Needham Heights, MA: Allyn & Bacon.

Buckley, A. (2000). Multicultural reflection. *Journal of Teacher Education, 51,* 143–148.

Clark, C., & O'Donnell, J. (1999). Rearticulating a racial identity: Creating oppositional spaces to fight for equality and social justice. In C. Clark & J. O'Donnell (Eds.), *Becoming and unbecoming White: Owning and disowning a racial identity* (pp. 1–9). Westport, CT: Bergin & Garvey.

Connell, R. W. (1994). Poverty and education. *Harvard Educational Review, 64*(2), 125–149.

Dilg, M. (1999). *Race and culture in the classroom: Teaching and learning through multicultural education.* New York: Teacher's College Press.

Emerson, R. M., Fretz, R. I., & Shaw, L. L. (1998). *Writing ethnographic field notes.* Chicago: University of Chicago Press.

Goetz, J. P., & LeCompte, M. D. (1984). *Ethnography and qualitative design in educational research.* Orlando, FL: Academic Press.

Gomez, M. L. (1994). Teacher education reform and prospective teachers' perspectives on teaching "other people's" children. *Teaching and Teacher Education, 10*(3).

Goodwin, A. L. (1994). Making the transition from self to other: What do preservice teachers really think about multicultural education? *Journal of Teacher Education, 45,* 119–131.

Grant, C. A., & Koskela, R. A. (1986). Education that is multicultural and the relationship between preservice campus learning and field experiences. *Journal of Educational Research, 79*(4), 197-204.

Greenman, N. P., & Kemmel, E. B. (1995). The road to multicultural education: Potholes of resistance. *Journal of Teacher Education, 46,* 360–368.

Hay, R. (2003). *Virtual conversations: The use of Internet based synchronous chat in basic writing.* Available at http://www.cwrl.utexas.edu/currents/fall03/hay.html

Helms, J. (1993). *Black and white racial identity.* New York: Praeger.

Horton, J. K. (2002). Learner Diversity Spring Syllabus 2002. Retrieved September 30, 2002, from learner Div. Website. http://classdat.rcoe.appstate.edu/CI/hortonjk/ci3000/30002002.html

Houser, N. O. (1996). Multicultural education for the dominant culture: Toward the development of a multicultural sense of self. *Urban Education, 31,* 125–148.

Irvine, J. J., & Armento, B. J. (2001). *Culturally responsive teaching: Lesson planning for elementary and middle grades.* Boston: McGraw-Hill.

King, J. (1991). Dysconscious racism: Ideology, identity and the miseducation of teachers. *Journal of Negro Education, 60*(2), 133–146.

Ladson-Billings, G. (1994). *The dreamkeepers.* San Francisco: Jossey-Bass.

Larkin, J. M. (1995). Curriculum themes and issues in multicultural teacher education programs. In J. M. Larkin & C. E. Sleeter (Eds.), *Developing multicultural teacher education curricula* (pp. 1–16). Albany: State University of New York Press.

Lima, E. S., & Lima, M. G. (1998). Identity, cultural diversity and education: Notes toward a pedagogy of the excluded. In Y. Zore & E. T. Trueba (Eds.), *Ethnic identity and power: Cultural context of political action in school and society* (pp. 321–343). Albany: State University of New York Press.

Lopez, I. F. H. (1996). *White by law: The legal construction of race.* New York: New York University Press.

McCarthy, C. (1994). Multicultural discourses and curriculum reform: A critical perspective. *Educational Theory, 44*(1), 81-98.

McIntosh, P. (1989, July/August). White privilege: Unpacking the invisible knapsack. *Peace and Freedom,* pp. 10-12.

New, C. A. (1995). Oral histories: An interactive link in teaching language arts. In J. M. Larkin & C. E. Sleeter (Eds.), *Developing multicultural teacher education curricula* (pp. 105-114). Albany: State University of New York Press.

Quintanar-Sarellana, R. (1997). Culturally relevant teacher preparation and teachers' perceptions of the language and culture of linguistic minority students. In. J. Banks (Ed.), *Preparing teachers for cultural diversity* (pp. 40-52). New York: Teachers College Press.

Ramsey, P. G. (1998). *Teaching and learning in a diverse world.* New York: Teachers College Press.

Reich College of Education. (2000). Unit Plan 2000-2005. Retrieved March 2002, from Strategic Planning Statement Web site: http://www.ced.appstate.edu/facultystaff/unit_plan_2005.aspx

Retish, P., & Kavanaugh, P. (1992). Myth: America's public schools are educating Mexican American students. *Journal of Multicultural Counseling and Development, 20,* 89-96.

Rodriguez, A. J. (1993). A dose of reality: Understanding the origin of the theory/practice dichotomy in teacher education from the students' point of view. *Journal of Teacher Education, 44,* 213-222.

Spradley, J. P. (1979). *The ethnographic interview.* New York: Holt, Rinehart & Winston.

Stuart, C., & Thurlow, D. (2000). Making it their own: Preservice teachers' expectations, beliefs, and classroom practices. *Journal of Teacher Education, 51,* 113-121.

Tatum, B. (1999). Lighting candles in the dark: One black woman's response to White antiracist narratives. In C. Clark & J. O'Donnell (Eds.), *Becoming and unbecoming White: Owning and disowning a racial identity* (pp. 56–63). Westport, CT: Bergin & Garvey.

Valencia, R. R. (1991). The plight of Chicano students: An overview of schooling conditions and outcomes. In R. R. Valencia (Ed.), *Chicano school failure and success: Research and policy agendas for the 1990s* (pp. 3-26). London: Falmer.

Williams, H. (2003). *Appalachian State University student enrollment and faculty employment percentages by race.* Retrieved August 5, 2003, from http://www.diversity.appstate.edu/percentages.html#student

Zeichner, K. M., & Liston, D. P. (1996). *Reflective teaching: An introduction.* Mahwah, NJ: Lawrence Erlbaum Associates.

10

THE ENGLISH-LANGUAGE LEARNER, THE TEACHABLE MOMENT, AND EMERGING TECHNOLOGIES

Linda C. Pacifici

Carmel J. Vaccare

Editor's note: This chapter discusses the teachable moment that will enable classroom teachers to find new ways to use technologies for instruction as well as strategies for the English-language learners (ELL), a group so often forgotten. Pacifici and Vaccare address three distinct domains of knowledge: (a) the English-Language learner (ELL), (b) the teachable moment, and (c) emerging technologies. Each topic is of pertinent interest for the classroom teacher and, when considered in light of each other, creates insights for meeting the English-language learners' needs.

English-language learners (ELLs), the teachable moment, and emerging technologies compose an unlikely trio of concepts that become related in important ways. It is common knowledge that public school classrooms in the United States have become increasingly diverse, especially in ethnic-racial student enrollment (The Condition of Education, 2000). The transformative potential of technology in education has yet to be completely understood for its emerging implications as well as for its applications in the classroom (Reinking, 1998). The teachable moment, meanwhile, is an idea that remains obscure in educational conversations, yet can provide a lens through which to establish instructional integrity. Each of these topics stands alone as individual domain of knowledge in education. When brought together and examined in relation to each other, insights are highlighted that are important for classroom teachers and their ELLs. In this chapter, we first consider the classroom teacher and the learning needs of ELLs. We add the notion of the teachable moment and expand understandings of it with the added dimension of the ELLs. Last, we describe issues of emerging technologies in light of the classroom teacher, ELLs, and the teachable moment.

ENGLISH-LANGUAGE LEARNERS

Hispanic students are the fastest growing student group in elementary and secondary schools (The Condition of Education, 2000), yet teaching the ELLs is difficult for monolingual mainstream classroom teachers who lack English-as-a-Second Language (ESL) training (Schwarzer, 2001). More than 25% of classroom teachers have ELLs in their classrooms, yet 70% say they have no ESL academic training. Developing a culturally sensitive pedagogy supports both classroom teachers and ELLs (Rolon, 2004; Smith, 2004). Culturally sensitive pedagogy involves teachers embracing a stance of curiosity and inquiry for themselves about their ELLs (Smith, 2004). In addition to learning about these students' home cultures, a positive learning environment is enhanced through teachers gaining the following information about their students: (a) the differences in each student's previous schooling opportunities to develop school-based language and literacy; (b) understanding the family backgrounds of students in terms of socioeconomic status (SES) the conditions under which they emigrated, the degree of contact with home country, and the parental expectations for their child's academic achievement; and (c) ELLs interests, habits, and attitudes toward the acquisition of English (Smith, 2004).

It is crucial that teachers reflect about and acknowledge the pervasive deficit orientation that emphasizes what ELLs do not have in terms of English-language proficiency and schooling skills (Rolon, 2004). Incorporating an additive and inclusive approach enables teachers to maintain high learning expectations for ELLs and to find ways for including students as valued members of their classroom and school. Many strategies and approaches that work well for primary English-speaking students will also work well for ELLs (Smith, 2004). Teachers can review their best practices and include them in their everyday teaching because, "Good teaching is teaching for all. These strategies will help the English language learner and help typical learners as well" (Drucker, 2003, p. 22).

The ELL learns English in school to participate both in activities embedded in the social school settings as well as developing "academic proficiency": two different languages or discourses (Drucker, 2003, p. 23). ELLs find they use conversational English when engaging in social situations in school, such as conversations with other students, when playing on the playground, or asking teachers questions. They also need to understand academic English to learn curriculum content and skills. Thus, the classroom context is essential for ELL, especially for academic English: "In conversation, the setting, body language, facial expressions, gestures, intonation and a variety of other cues help ELL understand meaning. Academic English has fewer cues" (Drucker, 2003, p. 23).

Planning and creating contextual cues in the classroom for curriculum instruction begins with the development of a sense of classroom community for all students. Many student-centered strategies and approaches can facilitate ELL learning. These methods include paired reading, guided reading, partner work, small-group collaborative work, and choral readings (Drucker, 2003; Rolon, 2004; Smith, 2004). Embedding language focus lessons consisting of vocabulary and content concepts learning (i.e., relating and illustrating the concept of the American Civil War before studying it or reading a fiction trade book that includes the Civil War in its setting or theme) is important for both creating an inclusive classroom and for meeting the language learning needs of ELLs. Content area reading strategies and expository text reading strategies are excellent ways to include contextual cues in learning activities. These strategies include previewing text and the concepts in text before independent reading or application work, stimulating prior knowledge through modeling, creating links to students' home cultures, and providing graphic organizers and visuals for pre, during, and postreading activities (Drucker, 2003; Rolon, 2004; Smith, 2004). This brief overview of teaching and learning strategies works on the assumption that these methods serve to facilitate classroom community building as well as to create and sustain contextual cues in the classroom. As Smith (2004) pointed out, "Affective variables relate to the success in second language acquisition, and affective variables such as motivation, self-confidence, and commonsense should be encouraged in the classroom" (p. 49). We take the issues of community building, professional stance of inquiry, and classroom contextual cues to the teachable moment.

THE TEACHABLE MOMENT

Instruction in any setting traditionally involves the teacher, student, and content. The science of teaching has a long history of models, methods, strategies, skills, knowledge domains, and professional dispositions that seek to maximize student learning. So often the art of teaching is neglected in favor of traditional teaching practices based on teacher-centered, textbook-based teaching through the high-stakes standardized test-driven curriculum prevalent in current American schools. Every teacher understands that the prescribed methods cannot work without the qualities a teacher brings to the classroom. Qualities such as passion for the content area, love of seeing students learn, an intuitional sense about a student's level of engagement, and imagination of possibilities do not come from textbook teaching methods, models, or strategies. Similarly, student learning is not just demonstrated by test scores. These intangible qualities underlie the teachable moment, a concept often neglected in education. A conscious awareness of the role that imagination, need, desire, and interest play in the teachable moment can serve the classroom teacher who seeks to create effective classrooms for ELLs (Garrison, 1997).

As Garrison (1997) described:

> The "teachable moment" is perhaps the most sought after pedagogical prize. Every teacher knows what it feels like even if they cannot name its characteristics. It is as wonderful as it is elusive. We long for the moment when our class has that special quality of intimacy, openness, and creativity that provides us with the almost ineffable experience of getting through to our students, of connecting, and of our students learning and not just getting ready to take a test. All too often the moment slips away before we can seize it. The teachable moment comes so suddenly and departs so swiftly that many assume it is simply a gift of good fortune. (p. 115)

A teachable moment is ethereal yet tangible, identifiable yet elusive, sufficient but not necessary for learning to take place. It is not an instant but a period, not an endpoint but a continuum. The quest for a workable definition of this intangible feature is reductionist in nature, and the result is a compact definition.

The teachable moment is not serendipitous to the mind's eye in that it achieves what is consciously or unconsciously sought. Although serendipity can play a part in uncovering new paths and creating new insights, teachers can apply their stance of inquiry and community building for ELLs to facilitate teachable moments. Coupled with sensitivity to possibilities beyond what is known, a teacher has a chance to reproduce these moments. The unknown possibilities that are developed from the chaos of the moment can result in a teachable moment. Garrison (1997) explained:

> Imagination enables the search for ideas that can possibly reconstruct the situation. It takes the context and its "data," including emotional sympathetic data, as intuited and determined by selective interests and transforms them into a plan of action, an idea that if acted upon might allow the agent to achieve the desired ideal in realty. (p. 96)

The teachable moment is synchronistic in that teacher and pupil come together with all that is needed at a point in time that becomes a process of awakening insights and understanding. It is this synchronicity that is fundamental to the discussion. Although a moment can be a point in time, it may also be a period of time. The student and teacher arrive at a point in time, but their interaction takes place during a period of time. That their interaction may result in discrete insights or may be a continuously insightful process depends on internal factors that coincide with each other. A student can have insight in reading a book or seeing a play. A student can have many learning experiences without a teacher. For academic learning, with its lack of contextual cues, especially content knowledge and information, a teacher is necessary but not sufficient. The teachable moment is a case of the whole becoming larger than the sum of the parts.

The process of interaction between teacher and student creates a synergy that overcomes the barriers of preconstructed knowledge to produce insight and understanding. It is not merely the maximum amount of insight and understanding possible for a given moment. It is the maximum amount of insight and understanding possible at that moment. It is not the maximum amount of insight and understanding that is possible; it goes beyond preconceived intentions and expectations. Teaching with and for ELLs adds a dimension that applies to enriched dynamic teaching: The classroom context is fertile through the teacher's passion of inquiry and imaginative sense of possibilities. Teachers enact their professional disposition toward discovery of their ELL needs as, "Personal need, desire, and interest internally motivate the exploration. Imagination facilitates the inquiry" (Garrison, 1997, p. 117).

Any attempt to convey the fundamental character of an intangible results in a deficient definition. Defining a teachable moment is such a case. From previous discussion of a teachable moment, the definition must be temporal in phrasing and contain at a minimum: a teacher, a student, an interaction, and conditions of "need, feeling, imagination, paradox and possibility" (Garrison, 1997, p. 117).

The teachable moment is the interaction between student and teacher that both contains and results in the maximum insight and understanding possible at that moment. Sensitivity to the possibilities of the teachable moment parallels the teacher's intentions with ELLs. A positive environment is created when the teacher adopts a professional stance of personal inquiry for herself and her ELLs, " . . . understanding 'teachable moments' to be times when spaces open for the students and teacher to interact in a synchronistic and dynamic rhythm" (Garrison, 1997, p. 122). Attunement to teachable moments can increase the positive, contextual, enriched environment that ELLs needs. We add the teachable moment to the mix of the ELL and move to emerging technologies.

EMERGING TECHNOLOGIES

Past and existing technologies create new possibilities for communication and information in the classroom as research reveals stories of students gaining new perspectives of themselves and their capabilities as well as offering teachers new ways to support teaching and learning (Male, 2003). Reinking (1998) wrote that electronic text has capabilities not so readily available with printed text. These features include: (a) interactivity, (b) textual support for poor or developing readers, (c) multimedia integration, and (d) a fluid rather than fixed learning environment. Even with these opportunities, educators struggle with the impact of the latest emerging technologies on their students' lives as well as in the classroom. If "emerging devices, tools, media, and virtual environments offer opportunities for creating new types of learning communities for students and teachers" (Dede, 2004, p. 3), can teachers and ELLs benefit from emerging technologies in the classroom?

Technologies are always emerging. Interestingly, they are both a reflection of and a driving force in society. Although the apparent rate of technological change in society is intimidating ("Can you program your VCR" has become "Can you use all of the features in your DVD player"), it is manageable. If it were not, the present state of innovation in business, industry, and the consumer marketplace could not and would not be sustained. People adapt to and profit from the changes, yet suffer from a gap in learning and integrating emerging technologies with existing routines. This is especially an issue in education across disciplines, with teachers comfortable in using existing technologies that are displaced or supplanted by new technologies. For example, the overhead projector gives way to the LCD projector with Powerpoint™ for enhancing direct instruction. Meanwhile the Internet provides a parallel path to an extensive array of knowledge at one's virtual fingertips (as long as the network stays up).

Technologies used for instruction have developed over time in an evolutionary manner. The erasable writing marker and whiteboard is an adaptation of chalk on the blackboard, while chalk on the blackboard is several generations removed from primitive stick drawings in dirt. Filmstrips have evolved to videotapes to laser discs to CDs and DVDs, and to streaming video via the Internet. Recently, however, student/teacher and student/student communication has moved from face-to-face interaction, the ideal of a student and teacher sharing a bench (Garfield, 1871; cited in Hinsdale, 1971), to Internet chatrooms, videoconferencing over the Internet, and interactions and entire learning communities in virtual spaces by way of distributed learning communities (Dede, 2004). The latest generation of cell phones can access the Internet and, therefore, more dictionaries, encyclopedias, books, and resources than can be physically located in any school library. Additionally, students during a school day move back and forth between a world of instantaneous communication on their cell phones, capable of connections to any other phone in the world, to self-contained classrooms with filtered and restricted computer and Internet access.

Emerging technologies in certain instances may require shifts from the traditional passive learner roles with teacher as transmitter of knowledge to the teacher as facilitator of networked communities in asynchronous environments (Facemyer, 2004). Consider the use of an organized multi-user, object-oriented (MOO) environment in an eighth-grade classroom, where students discuss literature with undergraduate preservice teachers in a virtual dining room in a virtual house through a WebPal Project (Carico & Logan, 2004). The classroom teacher prepared the students with prereading activities, during reading with e-mail conversations, and organized the MOO topics. Yet the students co-constructed their own knowledge and meanings of text in this example of an emerging technology learning environment and community.

The community-building features of emerging technologies extend the teacher as facilitator of learning. Noting the lack of spontaneous, "serendipitous" interactions in a distance education community, Riedl (2004) described the use of a three dimensional virtual world in a graduate instructional technology program. He wrote:

> There has been much written about the importance of developing a sense of community among learners in distance education. Web-based discussions, chats, and other online tools provide opportunities to interact and share among distance education students and a sense of community can develop. But, the distance education environment affords little chance for serendipitous interactions that, it seems to us, are an important part of community. . . . We are seeking a means by which we can provide opportunities for a full and rich community of

learners, including opportunities for chance meetings among students from different classes or cohorts and between faculty and students who may not be in their classes at the moment. (p. 1)

These two examples of interactions in a virtual world by way of the Internet demonstrate "playing with" (Riedl, 2004, p. 1) emerging technologies where need, interest, and imagination motivate the inquiry. Community-building possibilities for the classroom teacher and ELLs open as:

the culture of the Internet allows you to link, lurk, and learn. Once you lurk you can pick up the genre of that community, and you can move from the periphery to the center safely asking a question—sometimes more safely virtually than physically—and then back out again. (Brown, cited in Williams, 2004, p. 2)

Plato illustrates our present-day limitations of understanding and utilizing emerging technologies when he recorded Socrates' concerns with the effects of writing, an emerging technology in his time in history:

For this invention of yours will produce forgetfulness in the minds of those who learn it, by causing them to neglect their memory, inas-much as, from their confidence in writing, they will recollect by the external aid of foreign symbols, and not by the internal use of their own faculties. Your discovery, therefore, is a medicine not for memory, but for recollection, for recalling to, not for keeping in mind. (http://www.bartleby.com/66/74/44574.html)

The desire to use a particular technology or the availability of a given tech-nology should not govern its use in instruction. By first framing what is pedagogically necessary, the appropriate technology can then be mapped to an instructional event. This is not to say there will always be an existing technology that will satisfy the pedagogy. It is to say that an inappropriate technology, or a compromise as to what is pedagogically necessary, needs to be properly identified. Therefore, using an inappropriate technology for instructional purposes could be more damaging than reliance on an exist-ing technology already in place by teachers.

One way to work with the application or relevance of a new technolo-gy for teaching is to use rubrics to evaluate the technological tool. Time, place dependencies, and degree of interaction compose one set of suggest-ed criteria to use when considering new technologies (Vaccare & Sherman, 2001). The emerging technologies rubric is a practical tool for emerging technologies.

EMERGING TECHNOLOGIES RUBRIC

Mapping existing technologies to pedagogical necessities is a persistent problem that begs this question: What can be generalized for nonexistent technologies that will emerge? A rubric of criteria used to consider technologies in educational settings establishes a baseline to be reconsidered in light of all present and future technologies. One set of factors to consider when mapping a new technology to an instructional activity includes the following: (a) place, (b) time dependencies, and (c) desired degree of interaction.

Place

Place and time are interrelated in terms of what is possible with instruction. How a technology liberates or constrains time and place determines how it is used for instruction. The most resource-intensive instructional activities are synchronous and place-bound (e.g., a class that meets on a regular basis in the same room, same building, face to face with teacher and students). The cost of transporting and coordinating the activities of a group of people in a building that is temperature controlled and physically maintained is an expensive proposition. The construction and layout of a room can have a profound effect on what types of educational experiences are either facilitated or constrained.

Teachers traditionally work face to face and are able to adjust instruction based on verbal and nonverbal cues. Although media comparison studies have shown that there is no significant difference in how instruction is delivered (Clark, 1991, 1994), research on ELLs' learning reveals the need for visual cues in the classroom. The advent of virtual online communities interacting in virtual worlds creates the need for teachers trained to teach and evaluate students in face-to-face instruction to learn new ways of mediating technologies supporting instruction. However, it would appear that a rational judgment of a technologies' worth should be on a change in resources, a change in access, or a change in immediacy of response. Does the technology liberate a student to present or interact in real time independent of where the other students or faculty are present that their knowledge or competencies can be assessed? Or does the technology require everyone to be colocated, constrained to be present in the same place, but liberated in access to other resources? These are many questions to ask of a technology and whether it is worth investing in instructional development time in its application.

Laboratories for science, language, and computers with licensed or proprietary software are place-bound. Examples of place-inhibited technologies beyond the classroom walls are satellite-delivered content, which requires infrastructure and the Internet. Although the Internet would at first blush appear to remove the barrier of place, it does require access to computers (for now) and Internet connectivity. An increase in wireless Internet access possibilities and cellular phone connectivity will act to further reduce the barrier of place. The speed of the connection affects what is possible. Streaming media such as movies require more bandwidth than static Web pages. Interaction with and control of remote instruments or for conferencing requires low latency, the delay in response to an input, which are characteristics of particular types of connections. The constraints of place are basic in considering the impact of any technology to provide resources for spontaneous moments of learning connection.

Time

Technologies that free a teacher's time to personally interact with a student by offloading content delivery or otherwise engaging other students in a class are worth identifying and using. To this end, there are questions we can ask of any technology. Does the technology support students to experience the same event at the same time? Does it enhance the experience or enable access to the experience to those who would otherwise be denied it? Does a delivery mode merely duplicate the experience through a different system of resources? The capacity to immediately provide context, information, or experiences that can create a teachable moment must be available at the appropriate time that may approach us unawares (Garrison, 1997). Access to a technology at the right moment may make time the critical element in evaluating a technology's worth to contribute to a teachable moment.

Combining Time and Place

A guest lecturer or historical broadcast might dictate a dependency on time, whereas a class lecture may not require simultaneity, but may require discussion in real time. Lab equipment or a museum creates experiences that are place-bound, although not always time constrained. Technologies can be assessed as to their capacity to be accessed in a variety places and/or times. A map (see Fig. 10.1) for logically dividing technologies, delivery modes, or instructional necessities enables a filtering process for technology characteristics. As technologies emerge, they can be analyzed for their capacities to transcend time and place or their limitations constrained to time and place.

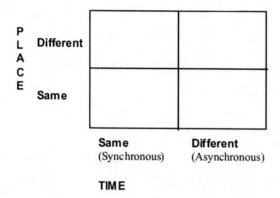

Figure 10.1. Time and place quadrants (Coldeway, 1986).

INTERACTION

How a technology supports or changes communication and interaction between teacher and students is a fundamental concern to more than the social constructivist or those who are concerned with developing a learning community. As the notions of learning are affected by technologies, the nature of interaction is also changed. A technology's support of interaction is another filter for analyzing emerging technologies.

The instructional argument for moving from a satellite distribution of lectures to interactive videoconferencing was increased interaction between students and teacher. The cost shifting from paying for satellite transmission costs to increasing network bandwidth had a greater affect on the amount of Internet capacity than on the actual number of courses delivered through this medium. A shift in the delivery model enabled an infrastructure for asynchronous delivery of courses and access to resources. That translates into an expansion of the times that a student may experience a learning community.

A technology that supports real-time interaction can be viewed as a semi-permeable membrane—some information passes and some is blocked. In the case of interactive videoconferencing, it can be as simple as what the camera is focused on as opposed to what occurs off camera. Virtual presence should be evaluated not for equivalence with face to face, but rather the level and immediacy of any interaction. Does it support simultaneous interaction for more than two people? Immediate and appropriate response can dictate real-time interaction, whereas delaying response can promote reflection. In the first case, a teachable moment depends on communication, whereas the second case depends on designing the possibility of an appropriate stimulus for a teachable moment. Yet we assume that the common denominator for teachable moments is the immediacy of interaction. There is a tension in defining teachable moments as requiring a stimulus or as arising from an ill-defined nexus of interactions.

Feedback

A technology can be passive as in a book—where a reader cannot interrogate and probe, but must infer or extrapolate based on internal knowledge or other sources. This can be taken as no interaction (Fig. 10.2). A technology can support interaction as either a conduit (telephone, e-mail, videoconferencing, etc.) or an external source as in computer-based instruction (CBI). As a conduit between people, the technology can assist in moving within Vygotsky's (1978) Zone of Proximal Development. Interaction implies feedback, which can alter the direction or scope of communication and therefore movement in socially constructed environments. But does this extend to technology as a prime mover for intelligent interaction because technologies can provide dynamic feedback? (Vaccare & Sherman, 2001).

Interactivity implies feedback (see Fig. 10.3). That feedback can be regenerative, positive, or degenerative, negative. The immediacy of the feedback supported by any interactive technology has a direct bearing on a learner and the possibilities of teachable moments.

The behaviorist view is that feedback serves as reinforcement, whereas the cognitivist view is that feedback eliminates errors in conceptualization (Mory, 1996). Emerging technologies of MOOs and other distributed online communities (Dede, 2004; Riedl, 2004) embrace a social constructivist orientation, in which the individual brings internal knowledge and contexts to an interactive instructional event. As multiple forms of interaction are introduced, the options for discussion and interpretation increase. In current CBI, the interaction and feedback are limited to predetermined programmed interactions and feedback. When the capacity for interactions with other people is introduced, the possibilities and directions for context

Internal Sources	External Sources
Individual Contexts	Stimuli
Self-contained	Other People
	"Intelligent" Technology

Figure. 10.2.   Brown scale modified by Sherman for the degree of interaction (Vaccare & Sherman, 2001).

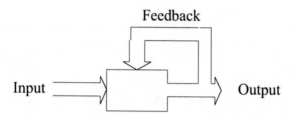

Figure 10.3.   Feedback loop.

and movement in the Zone of Proximal Development are greatly enhanced (Vygotsky, 1978).

The Socratic method is an example of feedback in an instructional mode. Responses to questions provide information that is used to form subsequent questions. This question–response process is a continually evolving feedback loop. If a computer were capable of this form of interaction, a facilitator or instructor would not have to be available for synchronous interaction.

Mapping Time, Place, and Interactivity

Time, place, and interactivity can be modeled as a three-dimensional space where a technology can be located as to its degrees of freedom (Fig. 10.4). A given technology can overlap or fill the space as to the capabilities to transcend time and place constraints and to support any level of interactivity.

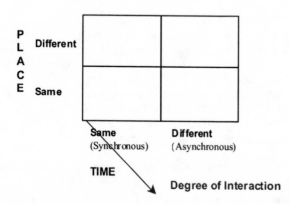

Figure 10.4.   Integration of time, place, and degree of interaction.

Mapping technologies according to their capabilities to either constrain or to liberate learners in place, time, and capacity to interact allows one to get a handle on emerging tools and their place in instruction.

CONCLUSIONS

Teachers learn how to meet ELLs' learning needs just as they must also learn to select and use emerging technologies as learning tools. Teachers learn to reframe effective strategies to use with ELLs and in the same manner learn to reframe ways to incorporate emerging technological tools as learning activities. Teachers first engage in internal reflection on the enculturation of the deficit orientation toward ELLs and make changes to include these learners with the same expectations they have for primary English-speaking students. In the same manner, teachers develop their orientations about technologies and the possibilities in the classroom. Both endeavors work toward the dual goals of building community for all students while maintaining rich contextual cues for ELLs. The qualities that underlie the teachable moment work simultaneously for teachers to rethink both ELLs as well as emerging technologies. The emerging technology rubric applies logic to the ill-defined possibilities, whereas passion, need, interest, and imagination provide a release from the tensions and pressures of external evaluations. These internal qualities can feed and supply teachers' ideas for instruction.

REFERENCES

Carico, K., & Logan, D. (2004). A generation in cyberspace: Engaging readers through online discussions. *Language Arts, 81*(4), 293-302.

Clark, R. (1994). Media will never influence learning. *Educational Technology Research and Development, 42*(2), 21-29.

Clark, R. E. (1991). When researchers swim upstream: Reflections on an unpopular argument about learning from media. *Educational Technology, 3*(2), 34-40.

Coldeway, D. O. (1986). Learner characteristics and success. In I. Mugridge & D. Kaufman (Eds.), *Distance education in Canada* (pp. 81–93). London: Croom Helm.

The Condition of Education. (2000). *Racial-ethnic distribution of public school students*. National Center for Education Statistics Office of Educational Research & Improvement, U.S. Dept. of Education. Retrieved October 15, 2001, from http://nces.ed.gov/pubs2000/coe2000/section1/indicator4.html.

Dede, C. (2004). Distributed-learning communities as a model for educating teachers. In D. Willis (Ed.), *Proceedings of the Society for Information Technology & Teacher Education International Conference* (pp. 3-12). Norfolk, VA: AACE.

Drucker, M. (2003). What reading teachers should know about ESL learners. *The Reading Teacher, 57*(1), 22-29.

Facemyer, K. (2004). Asynchronicity: Distributed learning communities. *Virtual WSU*. Retrieved May 24, 2004, from http://www.wsu.edu/vwsu/direction/Direct papers/Asynchroncity.html/

Garrison, J. W. (1997). *Dewey and eros: Wisdom and desire in the art of teaching.* New York: Teachers College Press.

Hinsdale, B. A. (1971, December 28). *Garfield and education 1882.* Address to Williams College Alumni, NY.

Male, M. (2003). *Technology for inclusion: Meeting special needs of all students.* (4th ed.). Boston, MA: Allyn & Bacon.

Mory, E. H. (1996). Feedback research. In D. H. Jonassen (Ed.), *Educational communications and technology* (pp. 919–956). New York: Macmillan.

Reinking, D. (1998). Transforming texts. In D. Reinking, M. McKenna, L. Labbo, & R. Kieffer (Eds.), *Handbook of literacy and technology: Transformations in a post-typographic world.* Mahwah, NJ: Lawrence Erlbaum Associates.

Riedl, R. (2004). *Building a program in a virtual world.* Unpublished manuscript.

Rolon, C. (2004). Educating Latino students. In F. Schultz (Ed.), *Annual editions, multicultural education, 04/05.* Guilford, CT: McGraw-Hill/Dushkin.

Schwarzer, D. (2001). *Noah's ark: One child's voyage into multiliteracy.* Portsmouth, NH: Heinemann.

Smith, K. (2004). Language as we know it, literacy as we know it, and content area instruction: Conscious strategies for teachers. *Multicultural Education, 11*(4).

Vaccare, C., & Sherman, G. P. (2001). A pragmatic model for instructional technology selection. In R. M., & M. A. Fitzgerald (Eds.), *Educational media and technology yearbook* (pp. 16–23). Englewood, CO: Libraries Unlimited.

Vygotsky, L. S. (1978). *Mind in society: The development of higher psychological processes.* Cambridge, MA: Harvard University Press.

Williams, B. (2004). Participation in on-line courses—how essential is it? *International Forum of Educational Technology & Society Online Discussion.* Retrieved January 28, 2004, from http://ifets.ieee.org/discussions/discuss_january2004.html.

ABOUT THE AUTHORS

Alison Carr-Chellman is associate professor in charge of Instructional Systems at The Pennsylvania State University. She graduated from Syracuse and Indiana Universities. Her research interests include systems thinking, diffusion of innovations and technologies, and systemic change.

Davin Carr-Chellman is the Assistant Director of the Center for Ethics and Religious Affairs at The Pennsylvania State University. Currently a doctoral student in Adult Education, Davin's background is in Philosophy (BA, MA). His interests include the philosophical and empirical study of communities and the development of effective human agency within those communities.

John Hollenbeck teaches online learning and distance education at Old Dominion University. His work centers on a critique of American higher education and the possibilities for reform through alternative technologies.

Julie Horton is an assistant professor at Appalachian State University in Boone, North Carolina. Her research interests center on issues of White identity and multicultural teacher education.

Robert Muffoletto is an associate professor of educational technology at Appalachian State University, College of Education. His inquires include the nature of knowledge and power in the use of technology in education, collaborative learning communities for online learning environments, and questions related to new media and global education.

Karen L. Murphy, Ed.D., is Associate Professor Emeritus at Texas A&M University and is currently Faculty Developer for online learning at Western New Mexico University. Research interests include sociocultural context of learning at a distance, online collaborative learning, and design of online instruction.

Linda Pacifici is an assistant professor in the Department of Curriculum & Instruction at Appalachian State University in Boone, North Carolina. Her research interests include teaching the English language learner, as well as issues of integrating technology in instruction.

Lizzette Rivera, M.A., is an instructor at Lamar Institute of Technology and a doctoral candidate in Educational Technology at Texas A&M University. Previously, she was assistant professor at Inter American University of Puerto Rico. Research interests are computer literacy, Hispanic education, and cultural issues.

Ellen Rose's publications on technology, pedagogy, and culture include *Hyper Texts: The Language and Culture of Educational Computing* (Althouse, 2000) and *User Error: Resisting Computer Culture* (Between the Lines, 2003). She holds the McCain-Aliant Telecom Professorship in Instructional Design and Multimedia at the University of New Brunswick, Canada, where she directs a graduate program in instruction design.

Dominic Scott is an assistant professor at Millersville University of Pennsylvania. He completed his Ph.D. at New Mexico State University where he studied at-risk Chicano youth attending an alternative school. He is interested in small learning communities, education as liberation and White identity development.

David Shutkin is an assistant professor of Education at John Carroll University where he teaches undergraduate and graduate courses in educational technology. In 1994, he received his Ph.D. from the University of Wisconsin in Curriculum and Instruction. His research concerns technology studies and nonfoundational ethics in education. At present, Shutkin is researching the recycling and demanufacturing of end-of-cycle educational technologies.

Carmel Vaccare is an assistant professor in the Department of Educational Studies at Radford University in Radford, Virginia. He teaches instructional technology courses and participates in a wide range of instructional technology projects in Virginia.

AUTHOR INDEX

SUBJECT INDEX

Printed in the United States
67554LVS00002B/1-48

9 781572 737402